TECHNIQUES OF PAINTING

HENRY GASSER, N.A.

 VAN NOSTRAND REINHOLD COMPANY

NEW YORK   CINCINNATI   TORONTO   LONDON   MELBOURNE

To my wife, Joane, whose help and

encouragement made this book possible.

VAN NOSTRAND REINHOLD COMPANY Regional Offices:
New York   Cincinnati   Chicago   Millbrae   Dallas

VAN NOSTRAND REINHOLD COMPANY Foreign Offices:
London   Toronto   Melbourne

Copyright © 1958 by REINHOLD BOOK CORPORATION
Library of Congress Catalog Card Number 58-10222

Published by VAN NOSTRAND REINHOLD COMPANY
450 West 33rd Street, New York, N.Y. 10001

16   15   14   13   12   11   10   9   8   7   6   5   4

TABLE OF CONTENTS

HENRY GASSER, N. A.

Born in Newark, N. J., Henry Gasser attended the Newark School of Fine and Industrial Art and the Grand Central School of Art. This was followed by study at the Art Students League of New York in the classes of Robert Brackman. He later studied privately under John R. Grabach. His paintings are in more than twenty-six museum collections including, the Philadelphia, Boston, and Newark Museums, the International Business Machine Collection, and the Historical Properties Section of the War Department. For more than twelve years his work has been exhibited throughout the United States and abroad, winning a number of important awards.

Among the awards that Henry Gasser has received are the Hallgarten prize at the National Academy; prizes at the American Water Color Society; the Connecticut Academy first and second prizes; the silver and gold medals at Oakland, California; the Allied Artists of America Gold Medal, and various awards from Audubon Artists, Salmagundi, Philadelphia, Baltimore, and Washington Water Color Clubs. He is a life member of the National Arts Club, the Grand Central Art Galleries and the Art Students League as well as a member of a number of other art organizations, including the National Academy of Design, American Water Color Society, Salmagundi Club, Philadelphia Water Color Club, Allied Artists of America, Baltimore Water Color Club, Audubon Artists, Connecticut Academy and New Jersey Water Color Society. He was elected a Fellow of the Royal Society of Arts in 1957.

Henry Gasser served as Director of the Newark School of Fine and Industrial Art from 1946-54 and is now lecturing and demonstrating painting techniques for art groups and schools in various parts of the country. He is the author of several books, including Oil Painting: Methods and Demonstrations, and Casein Painting: Methods and Demonstrations.

INTRODUCTION

Too many students limit themselves—and therefore their progress—to the obvious use of a medium. For figure studies they use only charcoal. The pencil they employ solely for sketching and for the preliminary planning on paper or canvas for the color that is to follow. For fine detail in line, pen and ink is their one medium. Brush and ink are strictly for broad handling. And so on.

These students often persist in this one-track attitude when they start using color. They think of watercolor in terms of a quick interpretation of the subject; pastel serves as the medium for subjects requiring delicate handling; and oil is the only proper medium for producing the "monumental" painting.

Much of the blame for this parochial approach can be laid to the art student's early training. There he concentrated mostly on learning the technique of handling the various mediums. The subjects selected were invariably those which were sympathetic to the mediums he was working with at the time. While a part of this book deals with techniques and the new methods that have been developed, it has a more important purpose. It endeavors to show how one medium helps another, from the germ of the idea to the finished painting.

The book is made up of eight chapters. The first chapter illustrates how the same subject can be interpreted in various ways: the arrangement of the light and dark patterns can be altered, different techniques can be used, the proportions of the picture can be changed to add impact to the subject, the mood can be varied. This chapter stresses the importance of seeing a subject in more than one way.

In the second chapter the approach to the subject is explored—whether it is to be in-terpreted in a detailed manner, handled freely, or rendered in a decorative style.

Figure composition, with emphasis on the importance of the figure in picture-making, is discussed in the third chapter.

The fourth chapter illustrates the use of the photograph as an aid to the artist.

Working with color, and technical demonstrations of direct painting, underpainting, glazing and imprimatura methods are illustrated in full color in the fifth chapter.

The author felt that, rather than having the usual large color plate illustrate the final results of a demonstration, far more information could be imparted by showing the various steps in full color. The handling of oil, watercolor, casein, charcoal, pastel, colored inks, and lesser known mediums ends this chapter.

The sixth chapter gives several case histories of prize-winning pictures and museum acquisitions. These illustrate how the methods in the previous sections of the book helped in developing the paintings.

In recognition of the increased popularity of murals for the home, the seventh chapter shows working methods for such painting.

Suggestions on how to present your picture conclude the book.

The author will be gratified beyond measure if this book leads student-readers to:

1. Paint several versions of the same subject until such concentration produces a well organized picture.

2. Search constantly for ways to strengthen the interpretation of a subject and to establish, through organization and design, an expression of a personal mood.

3. Cultivate a serious approach to their art and the mediums they use.

PICTURE PRELIMINARIES

How the same subject can be interpreted in many ways is featured in the first chapter of this book. Changing the arrangement, altering the shape of the picture, varying the mood, and even switching from one medium to another—all contribute to different interpretations of the subject.

But, probably, it is the way the subject is affected by the pattern of light and shade that creates the most impact upon the student. We have all experienced seeing subjects that seemed just ordinary. Then, one day, the same subject is seen under different lighting conditions. It might have been that it was viewed at a different time of day than usual. What was previously ordinary—almost dull—now becomes alive with a dramatic suddenness! Upon studying the subject, objects that were once isolated shapes are now knit together with interesting cast shadows. A larger object casts its shadow over a smaller object and the latter becomes a mysteriously beautiful note, forcing its color through the enveloping shadow. The light areas, previously washed out and faded, are now bathed in a warm glow. Here is something to paint and you wonder how you ever missed it!

It is this pleasing arrangement of light and shadow that the student must seek first. This applies to all subject matter—whether it is figure, still life or landscape. By discovering such an arrangement, the student will find it easier to sustain his interest until the subject is completed.

The rough sketches below illustrate, simply, how the arrangement of the light and dark pattern is changed as the source of light changes. Starting with #1, the light comes from the extreme left, casting elongated shadows. Then, as it comes around, the shadows become shorter. As the light encircles the houses, the shadows are reversed and gradually become longer again. Note, for example, how much more pleasing the shadows are to the arrangement of the houses in #5 as compared with #3. In the latter, each house becomes an isolated unit. The light areas of the houses are uninteresting and the shadows contribute little to the design pattern.

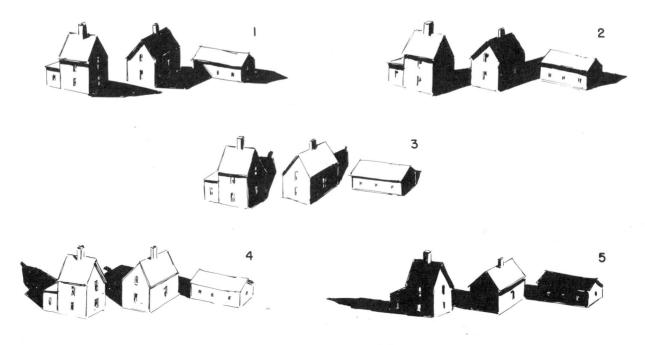

Once the best arrangement of light and shadow on the subject has been found, some preliminary planning of the composition is necessary. Shown above are notes typical of compositional roughs that you should make before starting a painting directly from nature. Make no attempt to show detail—indicate roughly only the main lines of the composition and the areas of light and dark. These drawings are not intended to delineate the numerous details of the subject; they are merely notes to achieve the most interesting arrangement preparatory to painting. The painting, in turn, is intended to be a color sketch of the subject.

However, if your color sketch turns out to have definite possibilities worth developing into a larger painting, then more detailed studies should be made. You may find it advisable to return to the spot to gather more data, particularly if the large painting is to be made in the studio.

There are artists who start and complete a large painting on the spot. At present, however, doing the finished painting in the studio is the most popular method of working. A compromise is to start the large painting directly from nature, achieving the color values in a rough manner, and then doing the necessary refining in the studio. If you follow this method, you should make detailed spot notes to supplement the painting for later reference.

In all probability you will find that the subject, your temperament, and the amount of knowledge you have accumulated tend to dictate the method you employ.

There are advantages and disadvantages in all of these methods. During your early years of study, I would advise you to paint as much as possible on the spot. Store up as much knowledge as you can through direct contact with nature. Then your later studio painting will be much more convincing.

INTERPRETATION OF THE SUBJECT

Below are two paintings which illustrate different interpretations of the same subject —a railroad station. The upper picture is an impression of the subject in its surroundings. It has not been singled out, being placed in the center of the row of buildings. However, in full color it does attain more prominence. The various placards are colorful and the large windows reflect varying colors from the buildings and objects across the street. The side of the adjacent building is made up of drab grays, which tend to enhance the color of the station and hold the viewer's eye on the center of interest.

The other picture could be termed a "portrait" of the station. Although the center of interest is flanked by buildings on either side, it is strengthened by revealing only a part of those buildings. As a final means of dispelling any doubt of its identification, its importance is stressed by the sharp lettering.

How you choose to interpret a subject is entirely a personal matter. The examples shown are only two of many possible.

An impression of the subject in its immediate surroundings.

A "portrait" of the subject.

8

SAME SUBJECT UNDER VARIOUS CONDITIONS

Several years ago, whenever the weather was unfavorable for outdoor work, I made sketches from a fellow artist's studio. On the right are three illustrations of such sketches: a rainy day, a night scene, and a snowfall.

The quiet and comfort of the studio lent itself well to concentrating on what I saw through the window. I was able to make exhaustive studies of the subject under all conditions. On a rainy day there was much to be learned about the importance of lost and found edges, restrained color, reflections, etc. The night scene revealed the wealth of color that exists in seemingly black shadows. Figures that appeared at first to be dark silhouettes were found to possess many subtle color transitions. The color quality of neon lights, in contrast to the illumination of the electric bulbs, took on a new significance. It became a matter of utmost importance to learn how to paint the effect of artificial light diffusing cast shadows! Observing and painting snow scenes from the studio window proved invaluable later in painting winter subjects on the spot. I found that many times an apparently grayish blue, pale sky actually possessed a color that could be attained by the addition of such seemingly unlikely colors as light red, raw sienna and umber. Further study revealed that the shaded areas of snow were far from the obvious blue and violet. Study the same subject around the clock. Paint it in the morning light and then do another painting in the late afternoon. Note how the varying light affects the mood of the subject. This constant observing and painting of the subject under various conditions will prove most helpful in your future work.

ANOTHER VERSION OF THE SAME SUBJECT

The most pleasing arrangement does not always make the most interesting composition. This seeming paradox is partly the result of viewing the subject at the same eye level during all of your preliminary sketches. Several factors contribute to the degree of the visual changes that take place. The distance from the subject and the size of the surrounding objects are the main factors. You will note that as you walk closer to the subject the angle of vision becomes more distorted. As you sit down the distortion becomes even more acute.

As a means of avoiding the ordinariness that takes place in many compositions, a degree of distortion may be desirable. You will find this approach of particular interest if you feel that your interpretation of the subject has become commonplace. This change in viewpoint will enable you to discover possibilities in subjects that in the past you thought uninteresting. Indeed, the duller the subject may seem, the greater the challenge to your ingenuity to make it exciting!

The subject is painted from a position far enough away to avoid any distortion.

By getting considerably closer, the immediate surroundings of subject become distorted.

IMPROVING COMPOSITION OF THE SAME SUBJECT

Frequently, while in the studio reviewing paintings that have been made directly from nature, the thought arises: "How can the composition be improved?" Elements that were painted as they related to each other on the spot, do not always present the best possibilities of the subject. Some redesigning is necessary to strengthen certain areas and subordinate others. A rearrangement of the cast shadows will often help, along with intensifying some color areas and subduing others. By repeating certain colors through-

out the composition you will help direct the viewer's eye to the center of interest. You may find it necessary to simplify shapes that effect the pattern of the painting. Whatever it might be, make a thorough study of the spot painting before recomposing it in your studio.

Although you may have made the usual preliminary compositional notes on the spot, the fact that you were working directly from nature limited you to a certain extent. That is understandable, for you were studying and, in order to get the most from nature, it was necessary to establish relationships to the best of your ability.

But back in the studio your concern is to make the best possible interpretation of the subject. You have already accumulated the knowledge from nature—you will not lose that. Now you are free to make whatever changes you think necessary to improve the subject. The reproductions below of the spot painting and the studio interpretation illustrate this point.

SAME SKETCH AS SOURCE FOR SEVERAL PICTURES

Many of us, when looking at a vista, have immediately noted how many compositions it is possible to extract from nature. In turn, to a lesser degree, that holds true of a drawing that envelopes a large area. The rough pencil sketch below is an example.

The sketch was made some time ago from a hilltop in Gloucester, Massachusetts. Some time later I was looking through my notebook for some material that could be developed into a studio painting. I came across this sketch and my first impulse was to use the entire composition for a painting. Upon studying it, however, I thought it might be an interesting experiment to see how many compositions I could obtain from a single sketch. The five paintings reproduced on the opposite page are the result of the experiment.

The painting in the upper left corner shows the first composition. Very little was rearranged and the only object removed was the telephone pole.

The next painting, on the right, required a little more searching. The extra effort was worthwhile, and I think that it is the best composition of the group.

The painting on the left of the second row was not as successful. The roof area is weak and needs more dark for contrast. Possibly, the area behind the roofs should be lowered in key. This would tend both to accent the roofs and hold the eye within the more vital picture area.

The next composition is a variation of the first painting; it lacks the pattern of light and shade that makes the first one more effective.

As a final experiment I painted the upright composition shown at the bottom of the page. The placing of the fence stretching across the entire width of the picture is an obvious weakness. An improvised open gate would have helped the composition.

Incidentally, all of the paintings were done on a quarter-size sheet of watercolor paper. I find this size most convenient for general work. It is small enough to allow you to cover the area quickly for watercolor sketching, yet it is large enough to make detailed studies.

CHANGING PROPORTIONS FOR ADDED IMPACT

As the size of most paint boxes that the student acquires is 12 x 16 inches, he automatically does his outdoor painting on canvas panels that size, for they fit the box so conveniently. Since the panels fit in the box horizontally, the student generally paints a horizontal composition. Over a period of time it becomes a habit to paint landscapes in the same proportions and in horizontal positions.

This fact definitely limits the student's compositions, and, more important, it limits his way of seeing and expressing the greater possibilities of the subject.

Reproduced below is a small, spot sketch of a street scene in Paris. It is of a pleasing, but usual, proportion. Directly below the sketch is a studio painting of the same subject. I have made the composition about twice the width of the sketch, but have still retained the general aspect of the scene.

A certain number of changes will have to be made when you develop a sketch into a new proportion. Also, some subjects will require more improvising than others, but try to retain the character of the original sketch. You will find it a challenging exercise!

It is possible that what I have said about the habit-forming horizontal composition does not apply to you. On several occasions you have placed the canvas in an upright position and painted a vertical composition. Nevertheless, most of the time you will find that the vertical shape has been chosen as the subject, since skycrapers, tall steepled churches, etc., are more easily composed in this proportion.

Below is a spot sketch of such a subject. It is a street scene in Italy and the buildings fitted nicely into a vertical composition.

I recomposed the scene in my studio, elongating the proportions by doubling the depth but still retaining the same width. In this manner I was able to add more impact to the subject. For example, when I first saw the scene, the tall building in the center dwarfed the small newsstand in the lower right. Even the color relationship helped, as the building was a dull orange against the bright green newsstand.

When I made the studio painting I was able to stress this effect. Incidentally, even the color relationship was intensified—the small, bright green newsstand was an excellent foil for the large, dull orange building.

You may want to experiment with this elongating or stretching of the subject in some of your old sketches. You will find it fascinating and it will enliven or dramatize an otherwise ordinary subject.

EMPHASIS THROUGH SIZE AND SHAPE

On the opposite page are some experiments showing how, by simply cropping the picture, the center of interest can be emphasized or even changed.

The vertical picture at the upper left of the page is shown in its entirety. Then, a portion of the area on each side is cropped. The light in the water, guiding the eye to the bridge, is automatically given prominence. In turn, the bridge becomes important. By cropping the picture further, the light is intensified and the bridge is made even more prominent. Incidentally, the blue tone of the sky has lightened considerably in the reproduction. In the original painting the darker tone of the sky aids in emphasizing the glare of the water.

An example of changing the center of interest is demonstrated in the horizontal picture. Viewed in its entirety, the massive wall on the left side, combined with the arched wall on the right, conveys the heavy character of certain streets in Paris. Cropped on either side, as shown in the lower corner of the page, the heaviness starts to disappear. At the same time the figures and the lamp post attain greater prominence. (This is particularly true when viewed in full color.) Further cropping changes the picture completely. Now the figure of the woman and the lamp post have changed from secondary interest to a vital note in the picture.

By taking pieces of white cardboard and blocking off sections you can experiment in cropping some of your color or black and white sketches. New and exciting compositions may often be obtained through such experiments.

On the right is shown the full-sized painting. By cutting a piece of lightweight cardboard into two inverted "L" shapes, a flexible mat can be formed. The shapes are moved about the painting as illustrated, until a more pleasing composition is achieved.

In this example, the elimination of the sky and portions of each side and part of the base resulted in a more compact arrangement. By completely eliminating the sky, the light areas in the foreground and middle distance were emphasized. Watercolors that have not quite "come off" can frequently be salvaged by this method. The two inverted "L's" are placed in the position finally selected as an improvement over the original composition. A new mat is then cut to the size of the changed proportions.

VARIATIONS OF THE SAME SUBJECT

A few years ago I taught a summer course in landscape painting at the San Jose State College in California. While subject matter is abundant in California, the schedule did not allow sufficient time to travel any distance to obtain fresh, paintable material for the students.

I inquired if there was a local "motif" that we could paint and was informed that a nearby field with an old mill and some sheds was available. I gathered that the majority of the students were not too enthusiastic about doing the subject, as it evidently had been painted regularly each term. I thought that this might be an opportunity to show how a well-worn subject might be given a new lease on life by just changing the point of view, plus some slight improvising.

I made a series of small watercolors of the subject, changing the composition each time as I encircled the motif. Taking no more than fifteen minutes on each painting, I made about a dozen variations of the subject, seven of which are shown here. I took some liberties in varying the color schemes and moving an occasional mountain or tree about, but, in general, maintained the character of the subject.

At the conclusion of the demonstration I pointed out to the students that I had limited my compositions to a fixed rectangular proportion. Many more variations could be done by simply working in a vertical shape.

How much they gained from the lesson is problematical, but I learned that "by your students you are taught!"

CHANGE OF SEASON PRODUCES A NEW PICTURE

A shortage of sketching material on hand is a common complaint among students. After a season's accumulation of spot sketches, thought worthy of further development in the studio, have been exhausted, the question arises, "What to paint?"

I have found you do not necessarily have to restrict your studio painting to notes gathered on the spot. With imagination, sketches made during the summer can often be improvised into a winter scene. It must be assumed, however, that you have painted enough winter subjects directly from nature so that you can make the necessary changes with some authority. (See page 113.)

Below are shown two summer subjects that have been repainted in a winter setting.

The first example, the street scene, shows little change in composition in the conver-

sion. The sky has been darkened in the winter scene to accent the white of the snow, but the arrangement of the hanging wash, figure, etc., remain the same.

The subject matter has been rearranged in the other example. The trees in the foreground have been given more prominence and the size of the house reduced. I played up the evergreen trees in the middle distance and distant hills, because their dark green color made a good foil for the white snow. Moving clouds were improvised in the sky area to instill a dramatic quality to the scene. The original white surface of the paper was allowed to remain in the light areas of the house and snow. Try to hold such areas wherever possible when doing a snow scene. You will thereby impart a sparkling luminosity to your painting.

Many students start their career with the fixed purpose of painting in only one medium. While they may be required to work in many mediums during their art school training, invariably they find a single one that seems most sympathetic to their manner of working. This sympathetic rapport with one medium will undoubtedly hold true during their entire painting career and that is as it should be. However, as I mentioned in the introduction, one medium helps another. And you will certainly miss a lot of enjoyment if you do not experiment with the possibilities!

Many artists of the past, while they thought of themselves primarily as oil painters, also did etchings, lithographs, or watercolors for relaxation or commercial assignments. Whatever the purpose, they thought of these mediums in secondary terms. History has proven that it is the examples of these lesser mediums that hold many of these artists in high regard today. Even if the so-called secondary mediums have not been considered superior to their oil paintings, they have certainly contributed to their stature as artists.

It is true that various mediums do become labeled by the student as he progresses. When working in black and white, charcoal and pencil fall into the study group, in contrast to lithography, woodcuts, and etchings, which are classified in the craft category.

Subject matter can influence the medium

IN DIFFERENT MEDIUMS

chosen, and, if the subject is an assignment, technical requirements may dictate the medium to be used.

It is possible that many mediums can contribute to the creation of a picture, although only one will appear in the final painting. At the start, to get the idea of the picture on paper, mediums that can be handled in a broad manner, such as charcoal or pastel, can be used. This can be followed by planning one or several color schemes with a fast-drying medium, such as watercolor or casein. Once the composition and color scheme have been determined, drawings from life may be needed and you can then go back to charcoal. If you find that carefully delineated drawings are necessary, pen and ink or a hard lead pencil will be preferable. Then employ charcoal once more to compose the crystalizing idea on canvas, followed by the painting finally being completed with oil paint.

Again, several mediums can be used in a single picture, particularly in the field of illustration. Starting on an illustration board it is possible to employ pencil, charcoal, ink applied with both pen and brush, transparent watercolor, and opaque casein. Classified as "mixed media," all of them have played an important role in the final success of the picture. However, it is in the use of the medium as a form of expression complete in itself, that most artists receive their greatest satisfaction.

CHAPTER II

THE APPROACH TO
LANDSCAPE PAINTING

From Foreground to Background

Painting a landscape by individual planes is a method of simplifying the scene before you. It is not recommended as a regular painting procedure, but it is of help in reducing the confusion that so frequently besets a student when he is face to face with nature.

This breaking up of the planes can be accomplished in different ways. On the left the subject has been painted plane by plane, starting from the foreground and working back to the hills in the middle distance, then to the background and, finally, to the sky.

Quite a bit of study is required to determine each plane. It might be of help if you compare the scene before you to a stage setting. Each plane is a flat, with a certain amount of space between each plane.

PLANE-BY-PLANE METHOD

From Background to Foreground

We are now working in reverse of the previously described approach. After the sketch is made the sky is laid in, followed by the distant mountains.

Continue thinking in terms of a stage setting—the wings are represented by mountain area on either side, and the paper is gradually covered as we work toward the foreground. In both the fore-to-back and the back-to-fore method it is necessary to refine areas and add details and sharp accents wherever needed. This is done after all of the planes are painted.

As I mentioned, this is not a regular painting procedure. Actually, it is an exercise in simplification of depicting the various planes which may be helpful to the student.

23

THE DETAILED SUBJECT

Sooner or later in the student's art career he will have occasion to do a detailed subject. In all probability it will be an architectural subject in which he will be definitely limited in taking any artistic liberties.

If the subject is to be in color, watercolor allows far more drawing of detail before the application of color. After watercolor is applied, its transparent quality allows the drawing to show through. This enables the painter to control the situation at all times, as long as he keeps the color transparent.

In this demonstration the pencil drawing of the architectural detail has been done in a hard, sharp manner. A ruler was used at times to insure accuracy. When the paint was applied, the handling was relaxed a bit in order to avoid a cold, hard, final painting.

STEP 1. *A carefully detailed drawing is made of the subject.*

STEP 2. *A wash of light yellow is applied over the sunlit areas. While the wash is still wet, touches of darker yellow are floated over the light yellow wash in order to vary the tonal effect.*

STEP 3. *The shaded areas of the buildings are painted with washes of blues and violet. A division of the big masses of the warm and cool areas has now been established. This stage is concluded by returning to the warm areas. Washes of light red and orange are applied over the tree trunks and the pathway. The lawn is given a wash of light green.*

STEP 4. *The modeling of the trees and foliage on the side of the building is now rendered. This is followed by the painting of the cast shadows on the lawn and tree trunks. The sky showing through the trees and behind the buildings is then painted.*

STEP 5. *The figures, along with their cast shadows, are painted. The entire surface has now been covered, leaving only the details to be rendered. These are now done, along with some sharply painted accents, and the subject is complete.*

THE FREELY HANDLED SUBJECT

In contrast to the limitations imposed upon the painter in the previous section, the freely handled subject allows him his own interpretation of the subject.

Generally, the artist paints such subjects for his own satisfaction. They may be merely quick, impressionistic sketches, or studies of color effects in which the drawing is often of a distant secondary concern. Fleeting effects of light and dark, quickly changing weather effects, objects in motion, etc., are necessarily handled in a free manner in order to capture them on paper or canvas.

The medium selected has much to do with the results achieved. This is a case in which the more technical knowledge you possess of a particular medium, the freer you will be in handling the subject. While it is true that the student frequently obtains a simple free effect in his initial use of a new medium, it is an effect achieved through ignorance rather than knowledge!

Undoubtedly watercolor is the leading medium for obtaining accidental effects. This accounts for the fact that every so often important exhibitions accept an initial effort. "How naive" and "Charming simplicity" or "It's so sincere you can see the struggle!" may be the comments of the jury, but such accidents are not much help to the student.

It is true that our leading watercolorists frequently have "controlled" accidents where an exciting passage of color takes place through unusual blending. But that is only incidental to the over-all effect; it is still the design that makes their pictures important.

In the oil sketch on the left I concentrated only on the color effect. A drawing of details and composition can be done separately.

A sketching trip ended with the approach of a storm. The watercolor on the right was made in about ten minutes just as the storm broke.

STEP 1. *Omitting the usual pencil or charcoal preliminary drawing, the subject is roughly composed directly with paint.*

STEP 2. *Using plently of medium, the big masses are quickly painted in their approximate colors. The oil paint has been reduced to an almost watery consistency for fast handling.*

STEP 3. *Less medium is used as the painting progresses. By the time the painting is nearing completion the paint is applied at a normal consistency. In this final stage the color in the light areas is painted in an impasto manner.*

STEP 1. *As in the preceeding oil demonstration, the preliminary pencil planning is omitted and the subject is sketched directly with the brush. A blue color is used because any traces of the outline that may remain in the final painting will be harmonious with the atmospheric quality of an outdoor subject.*

STEP 2. *The background is quickly laid in, mixing the various colors directly on the paper rather than on the palette. Do not be too concerned with holding or blurring the preliminary blue outline. This stage is concluded with an indication of the color in the foreground.*

STEP 3. *The surface of the paper is gradually covered with color as foreground and middle distance are completed. When painting over an underlying wash that may still be wet, apply the color in a heavier manner. This is accomplished by using just enough water to make the paint workable. The heavy paint is easier to control and will not run so freely into the underpainting. The details are then painted and the subject is complete.*

THE VIGNETTE

The vignette is particularly effective when the subject is to be interpreted in a decorative or stylized manner. The apparent casualness of the tapering edges in the finished picture is often misleading to the student. Actually, the vignetted shape requires careful designing, and to be most effective the "lost and found" edges must be well planned.

The vignette lends itself equally well to a white or tinted background. The demonstration on the right has been done on *De Wint* watercolor paper. This paper, an antique gray color, is an excellent base when using casein or tempera paints. By varying the amount of paint and water, transparent and opaque color passages can be attained.

I have found that the vignette is best accomplished in the studio, using spot sketches for reference. The sketch below provided the subject for this demonstration.

The first step shows the penciled planning of the composition with vignetting indicated.

Step two commences with an application of clear water along the edges. The color is then floated in with the preliminary wash of water diluting it sufficiently to shade off gradually. The white house is painted opaquely.

The third step shows the paper gradually being covered, with the color passages painted either transparently or opaquely.

The final details are then painted to complete the vignette, as shown in step four.

CHAPTER III

FIGURE COMPOSITION

We have all seen painting in which the artist did an excellent job of the landscape, but the absence of life in the composition reduced its effectiveness. Or, again, the landscape was satisfactory but the figures were poorly rendered.

Drawing from life is an absolute must for the student. If he is to be successful, drawing from life will always be an important part of his artistic career.

It is not merely a case of being able to draw well enough to get by; you should receive constant enjoyment from drawing just for the pure sake of drawing. The life class during your student years will provide a foundation, but it is the constant observation and recording of figures you see every day that will be most rewarding. People at work, at play, walking, waiting for a bus, shopping, grouped at a corner—all are available for you to sketch.

Carry a small sketch pad with you at all times. With pencil or pen record the life around you. As the pads are filled, they will serve a twofold purpose. Your drawing will improve and you will build up an excellent source of material for studio paintings.

Below is an example of the use of such material. The woman sitting on the porch was the only figure that actually appeared at the time the color sketch was made. Later, when developing the composition for a studio

"Frog Hollow" — First Award, Springfield Art League

Sketch from life reproduced actual size.

painting, I thumbed through my sketch pads, looking for some figures that I felt would fit into the subject. The results are shown in the reproduction at left.

In addition to constantly recording figures you see every day, you should also make figure compositions on the spot. Although the continual movement of figures makes their incorporation into a composition difficult, the drawing of the figures in relation to their surroundings will be an invaluable reference aid in future picture making.

The subject reproduced above was painted in the studio from the black and white on-the-spot sketch shown in the right corner. While the figures were rearranged a bit in the painting, the sketch was followed fairly closely for the general composition.

This does not mean that you are restricted to following the spot composition in your studio painting. As you progress you will often combine parts of several spot compositions into the finished painting. You will find that your studio painting will possess

more life and authority when you can refer to such compositions.

You may still have to supplement certain details, such as the drawing of a head or hands, rearrange the distribution of light and shade. However, the relationship of the figures to one another, and in turn to their surroundings, is very important in figure composition and makes on-the-spot composing a vital necessity for the student.

FIGURE PAINTING ON THE SPOT

Probably most of the paintings in exhibitions with figures dominating the composition of an outdoor subject have been painted in the studio. To be able to paint such a subject convincingly in the studio means that much time has to be spent painting and observing figures in the open. While the pose can be simulated indoors, the color effects of natural light and striking the figure can be acquired only by direct study from nature.

On this page are shown studies that were made directly on the spot. In attempting to capture the quality of outdoor light and how the color of the various figures related to each other and their surroundings, I was not too concerned with the drawing. It was far more important to establish the color relationship; the drawing could be corrected later.

You might want to experiment with various color mediums when you do such work. Personally, I find that watercolor lends itself best for outdoor scenes. I can cover the paper faster and achieve the color effects quickly. While it is true that one color frequently runs into an adjoining one, I do not find this too upsetting. In many instances I believe that it helps the over-all effect by im-

Department of the Army's Art Collection

parting a loose, on-the-spot feeling to the subject.

However, oil paint may insure greater accuracy in obtaining subtle color effects. This is particularly true when doing heads and close-up details. You may find that by using plenty of mixing medium with the oil you can practically use a watercolor technique. Then, where more control is needed, use less medium. This will restore the heavier handling of the oil paint, enabling you to do as much subtle modeling as desired.

To ease my conscience when relaxing with television, I frequently make use of the sketch pad. Naturally, the constant movement on the screen allows you only to suggest the images before you, but it is surprising how your powers of observation can be developed. You can capture figures in motion, light-and-shade arrangements, and, if you have a flair for portraits, even likenesses or caricatures. Incidentally, I have found that televised opera is a particularly good source of material. The singers invariably return to the same pose and gestures when singing their arias. They may not be good actors, but they are wonderful models—and they sing beautifully!

PAINTING A SINGLE FIGURE

Starting with a single figure is the simplest approach when working with color. While oil paint may be an easier medium, in so far as making corrections, watercolor has many advantages.

A black and white sketch with color notations is used for the demonstration opposite.

I do not mean using direct watercolor, but rather a tinting, or filling in of areas over a pencil drawing. In this manner the drawing and the application of color can be accomplished in two stages. First, you can make the drawing in pencil with even some of the modeling depicted. When this is satisfactory, proceed into color. By keeping the watercolor transparent as you apply the washes, you can always use the underdrawing. Make corrections by using a stiff bristle brush to wash out any unwanted color areas which can then be repainted. The addition of Chinese White will make the color opaque. It should be used sparingly, or the charm of the transparency will be destroyed.

Shown at the upper left are the pencil drawings on watercolor paper. Directly below are some poses of the same model in color. These sketches are made about four to five inches in height. I would advise you to work fairly small in your initial attempts and thus avoid having to be too greatly concerned with details.

As you gain facility you may want to eliminate much of the penciled preliminary drawing. Then you will need only a rough pencil indication of the figure and depend upon the watercolor for color and modeling.

STEP 1. *A pencil drawing is made on watercolor paper indicating the figure and the main lines of the composition.*

STEP 2. *Starting with the sky, the areas surrounding the figure are painted. The latter is left untouched at this stage.*

STEP 3. *Working from light to dark, the figure and the base he is sitting on are painted. This is followed by the painting of the cast shadows. The details are rendered and an over-all checking is done to refine edges and color passages. Some sharp accents are added and the painting is complete.*

35

PAINTING A GROUP OF FIGURES

When you feel that you have progressed satisfactorily in doing a single figure you may want to try to compose a group of figures.

I had an opportunity to visit the locker room of a club where an amateur boxing tournament was to take place. As the fighters were getting ready for their bouts I made some quick fountain pen sketches, such as those shown below. At the same time I made mental notes of the various color schemes. I observed the relationship of one figure to another and how they formed into various groups. The cast shadows and the long row of olive-green lockers united these groups into an interrelated pattern.

For the next few days I thought of the picture possibilities of the subject. After making several small compositional roughs, I decided to do a large oil painting. Employing a model, I had him assume various poses that could be referred to in the subsequent painting. I then made a charcoal composition directly on the canvas. I had previously decided that the composition would be most effective in a proportion of about one to three, the height and width respectively. This emphasis on the width would lend itself well to the organization of the various figure groups that were to be incorporated into the over-all design.

The finished painting is shown at the bottom of the opposite page.

The spot sketches.

36

The studio drawings.

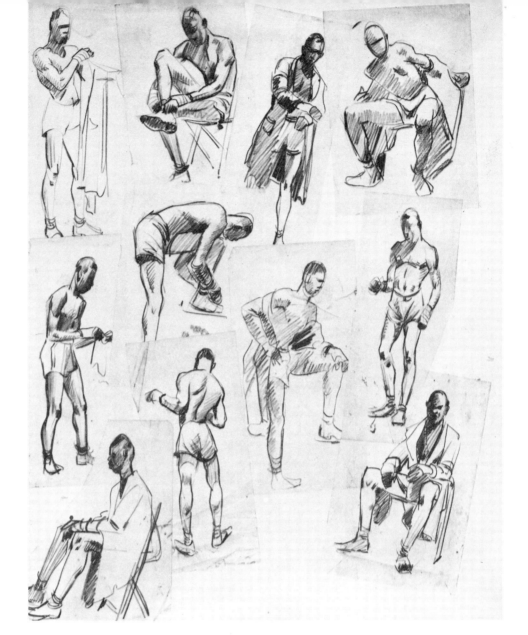

The finished painting.

PAINTING A STREET SCENE WITH FIGURES

In this chapter we will use a method that is of help in the placing of figures. It holds the drawing throughout the entire painting, reducing any repainting corrections to a minimum.

You make the usual pencil drawing and work on it until a satisfactory composition has been achieved. Then, instead of commencing with watercolor, you employ ink.

I have found that, while colored inks are not absolutely permanent, if you limit your palette there is small cause for concern. I use black with a bit of brown and neutral tint (the latter very sparingly).

The first stage in this method is shown below. The figures have been painted in mainly with black and brown ink, diluted with water. Every attempt has been made to keep the figures fluid. The paper is moistened with clear water in areas where a "lost and found" edge is desired. Frequently a stub pen instead of a small brush is used, to vary the line and texture. If the ink seems too heavy in a particular area, the pen is quickly dipped in and out a jar of clear water. This action is enough to dilute what ink remains on the point and the drawing is resumed. All of the figures and objects in the foreground are rendered in this manner at the end of this stage.

The second stage is shown on the opposite page. Still using the black and brown ink, supplemented with occasional touches of neutral tint, the background is suggested. I kept the paper constantly wet during this stage to blur the pen lines. When the ink drawing is dry, proceed to paint with transparent watercolor. The ink drawing now acts as an undertone, helping to model and impart a textural quality to the watercolor overpainting. The drawing remains undisturbed no matter how many subsequent color washes you apply over the ink undertone. The second stage concludes with the start of the transparent watercolor washes being applied.

In the third and last stage, the color

washes are continued until the entire drawing is covered. Wherever white areas are desired in the final painting the paper is left untouched. From now to the finish the color is refined and passages are intensified or reduced, as the case may be. It will be noted that where several washes have been applied the previously inked area may have dulled a bit. This may help in producing an atmospheric quality. However, if it seems too soft or grayed, you can sharpen it by using the ink again. Even though you may dilute the ink, keep a blotter handy to quickly blot and lighten any lines that become too dark.

PAINTING FIGURES IN A LANDSCAPE

In this demonstration the painting will be done with oil color. In many respects the handling of the figures should be less difficult than with watercolor. You can make changes and corrections more easily when working in oils, and alterations can be made at any stage without affecting the final painting.

The step-by-step demonstration shown on the opposite page is a typical procedure when painting in the studio from outdoor notes.

Not having any compositional sketches, I proceeded to make one from my notebook. I had observed a group of people on their way to a country church and thought that it had possibilities for a future painting. With these notes, as shown below, and the sketches of the surrounding terrain, pictured on the right, I started the composition.

Working with charcoal directly on the canvas, the composition finally evolved as shown in Step I. I lightly indicated the shaded areas and then sprayed the charcoal drawing with fixative.

Incidentally, in this stage the figures may become rather heavily outlined and stand out unduly. This happens if you make frequent changes when you are composing directly on

the canvas. As you redraw the various figures it is natural for the correcting charcoal lines to become darker and heavier. However, as soon as the toning process takes place (Step 2) you should blur or sharpen the lines where necessary.

The toning is generally started with a single color. While any color could be used, fairly fast drying color is technically better. Umber or Ultramarine are frequently used; the latter is particularly harmonious for landscape painting. Use a stiff bristle brush for toning, with little or no painting medium. Apply the paint as sparingly as possible, rubbing the tones on the canvas rather than brushing it on in a normal manner. When the canvas is covered, you will have estab-

lished an arrangement of the dark and light areas.

You can approach Step 3 in two ways. The color can be applied sparingly at the start, as in the toning process. Then, as the color scheme crystalizes, apply the paint in a heavier manner. Or you can paint the color in a direct, vigorous manner, using medium to keep your brush strokes fluid.

STEP 1. *A charcoal drawing is made directly on the canvas with the shaded areas indicated lightly.*

STEP 2. *Using a single color—one that is harmonious with the general color scheme—the drawing is solidified and the toning is done, preparatory to the application of full color.*

STEP 3. *As the toning process has been done in a thin manner, it is not necessary to wait for it to dry before using full color. Paint the darker areas first, gradually working up to the light. Once the entire surface is covered with paint, the desired degree of finish can then be determined.*

*Nautical
Details*

CHAPTER IV

THE PHOTOGRAPH AS AN
AID TO PICTURE MAKING

The photograph can be of great aid to the artist as long as he is aware of its limitations. It can be of much help as a means of recording data if there is not time to make a detailed drawing. A camera is a valuable piece of additional equipment when sketching in a foreign country. It will supply you with accurate reference when planning a studio painting from spot sketches. It is surprising how even a simple, black and white photograph will recall to mind the scene as it was at the time you made the sketch.

*Street
Scenes*

The photographs reproduced on this page are typical examples of valuable data. Nautical details, for example, are vital; even though they may be only roughly indicated in the studio painting, they must be correct.

In places where it is difficult to set up an easel—such as busy thoroughfares and industrial areas where it is impossible to get close to the subject, animals in motion, etc. —any important information you need can be recorded by camera.

*Various
Textures*

*Industrial
Scenes*

Transportation

Foreign Scenes

THE HUMAN EYE VS THE CAMERA EYE

Below is shown a photograph taken from the same spot where the pencil sketch was made. Note how the single eye of the camera has flattened the subject, particularly in the middle and background areas. See how the perspective of the road has been distorted—altered so much, in fact, that the curve has been completely lost. Again, note the recession that has taken place in the distant hills.

The fact of such distortions must be considered when using the photograph for reference. It also proves the artistic value of the most fragmentary sketch.

This particular photograph is of limited aid in developing a painting from the pencil sketch. It does show the anatomical details of the trees, and the textural quality of the hill on the left could be of use.

The photograph of the subject.

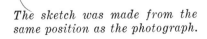
The sketch was made from the same position as the photograph.

43

PHOTOGRAPH AND SPOT SKETCHES COMBINED

The following is a case history of using a photograph when lack of time or equipment prevented a rendering of the subject.

While I was able to make some quick felt-pen sketches of the people around the bookstalls, I did not obtain a detailed drawing of the latter. However, I took a photograph for future data. Later, in the studio, using the photograph for reference, I made a rough indication of the bookstalls and selected some of the spot sketches of the figures to be placed in the composition. Finally, arriving at a suitable design, I painted a watercolor of the subject.

When working from a photograph, bear in mind that the camera distorts perspective. Note how the sharp recession of the bookstalls and the exaggerated width of the sidewalk has been resisted in the painting.

The Photograph

+

The Spot Sketches

=

The Finished Painting

PHOTOGRAPH AS AN AID FOR ARCHITECTURAL DETAILS

Undoubtedly the photograph is of great value in serving as an aid for architectural details. Even when you have the opportunity to make a careful pencil drawing, the photograph will help clarify many minute details when you paint the subject later.

The photograph below was taken at the same spot where the original drawing was done. In the case of an assignment that de-

mands an accurate rendering, it is wise to take additional photographs. Close-ups of areas that are difficult to discern from a distance will be helpful. Other angle views of the building will aid in establishing the depth of areas that are often difficult to determine from a head-on view. All of these will combine to make your rendering more convincing.

When comparing the photograph with the painting below, note how the latter has been elongated to compensate for the flattening effect of the photograph. A more majestic and impressive effect results. The clouds and the figures in the scene impart a feeling of life to the subject. This, combined with a rearrangement of the cast shadows, serves to sharpen the advantages of a painting as compared with a photograph.

THE PHOTOGRAPH SUGGESTS A PAINTABLE SUBJECT

At first glance the photograph reproduced at the right does not seem to be a particularly good subject for painting. It is lacking in pattern quality and the various shapes are delineated too vaguely. However, it is this very vagueness that makes the photograph an interesting exercise in creating a definite pattern.

Also shown is a rough black and white sketch that has been developed from the photograph. Halftone has deliberately been eliminated so that each element was reduced to a solid black and white pattern. The shapes were invented in the blurred areas of the photograph. Once a satisfactory design was established, I made a casein painting of the subject. Both the black and white sketch and the photograph were referred to as the painting progressed.

Incidentally, the photograph was taken in an area wherein I had been doing quite a bit of painting. This helped to simplify the painting problem, as I was familiar with the general over-all color effect.

COMPOSING FROM A PHOTOGRAPH

Occasionally you photograph a subject in which the distribution of the light and dark areas forms an excellent pattern. I believe that the snapshot reproduced on the left is a good example of this effect. The shadows cast from the awning and the balcony formed strong abstract shapes, in sharp contrast to the lace effect of the railing. Even the awning, which did not appear in the photograph, aided by casting its shadow in a vital area that needed a dark, balancing shape!

What I now needed was human interest. As the locale was New Orleans, the association with Mardi Gras was obvious. I made the group of thumbnail compositions by placing figures in various positions until I developed the painting shown below.

"Serenade to Joane"
Courtesy Grand Central Art Galleries

A COMPOSITE PHOTOGRAPH PRODUCES A VISTA

You may be interested in the following simple method of photographing a scene that envelopes an area too large to obtain in a single exposure.

Upon examining the photograph you will detect that two photographs were taken and then joined together. It was a simple matter to photograph first the area on the left; then, still standing in the same position, I shifted the camera a bit to the right and photographed the remaining one. Later, when the prints were developed, I placed them side by side. It required only a slight trimming to piece them together.

The photographic result does not have to be professionally perfect. All you are interested in is obtaining reference data for your painting.

"Gloucester Vista" — Courtesy A. Siminoff

The pencil drawing made from the composite photograph above.

The finished painting.

DEMONSTRATION OF WORKING
FROM A PHOTOGRAPH

On the right is the photograph that served as a guide for the demonstration below. A few changes have been made to improve the composition. A careful pencil drawing was made, indicating the various textures and the arrangement of light and shade. Note that, in the first color stage, the painting of the open window under the porch gives the key to the darkest note of the picture.

CHAPTER V

CHOOSING A MEDIUM FOR PAINTING ON-THE-SPOT

Probably the easiest way to decide what medium to use when painting on the spot is to choose the one with which you are most familiar. In working at home or in the classroom, oil paint is undoubtedly the most popular medium. The colors are first mixed on the palette, and when satisfactory, transferred to the canvas. Any mistakes that are made are easily corrected, and the most subtle tonal gradations can be worked on until the desired effect is achieved.

All of the above are good reasons for you to use oil color when first venturing into painting on the spot. Below is a typical example of an oil color sketch.

The drawing is secondary to the color, as it is for the latter that we have gone directly to nature to study. We are primarily in-terested in what takes place—how the light affects the color, how one color area is related to the adjoining color area, the subtle color variations within an area, etc. All of the studying necessary to solve these problems can be done with oil paint.

The 12 x 16 inch canvas panel that fits conveniently in the lid of the paint box is an excellent size for outdoor work. It is small enough to cover in a single painting session, yet large enough to let you obtain all the necessary details of the average subject.

However, you are not limited either by size or time when painting with oil. A larger canvas can be used, and, if the painting is not completed in one session, you can return to the spot the following day. This is, of course, only feasible if the light effect is

approximately the same as when the subject was started.

Along with your paint box you will need a sketching stool if you work seated. You can paint with the box resting in your lap, using the lid of the box as the easel. If you prefer to work standing, or if your canvas is large, you will need an outdoor easel.

Second in popularity, when painting on the spot, is watercolor. While color corrections are not as easily made as when working with oil, the painting is done faster.

Shown below are two versions of the same subject. While both mediums reveal a direct approach to the subject, the watercolor shows a crispness, which is characteristic of the medium.

It is in the painting of large areas, such as the sky, mountains, and the foreground, that watercolor can be applied more quickly than oil. Of course, it is necessary to allow time for watercolor washes to dry, but another section of the subject can be worked on during this drying process.

It takes experience to be able to judge how strong the wash must be when applying watercolor, to allow for loss of color when the painted area dries. This problem does not arise when painting with oil.

Watercolor also requires more accuracy in handling. Often an object may have to be drawn, the color applied, and the correct tonal values added—all in one operation.

Experiment with both mediums. It may be that the subject matter or its mood will determine which medium you will use.

The step-by-step process of painting the same subject in watercolor and in oil are shown here. I believe that illustrating the progressive stages in full color will enable the student to grasp the approach of each medium faster than with words.

The subject, shown at left, is painted in watercolor in six stages. Each stage depicts the vital changes that take place from the pencil drawing to the completion of the painting.

Starting at the left corner, and working down, the first stage shows the pencil drawing with the sky already painted.

When using watercolor, the sky is generally painted in one direct operation. The foreground follows, painted in flat washes. The painting continues, with some areas modeled where feasible. Gradually the entire surface of the paper is covered. Wherever a wash has to be painted over a previously painted area, it is done with a full brush in a deft manner. This will prevent disturbing the under color. It is when the first color wash is disturbed and mixes with the subsequent wash, that a muddy look results.

Sharp accents and the painting of details complete the watercolor painting.

On this page we see the three vital stages of the subject in oil paint. After the subject has been sketched with charcoal or pencil, a lay-in immediately establishes the light and dark pattern of the subject.

The lay-in can be made with any fast-drying color. I prefer using a blue, as it is both fast-drying and generally harmonious with an outdoor subject. The next step shows the color painted first in the dark areas and gradually worked into the light areas. The paint is applied in a sketchy manner.

As the painting progresses the canvas is gradually covered. Then, as one area is checked against another and corrections are made, the paint is applied more heavily. The subject is complete with the painting of details.

53

DIRECT PAINTING IN OIL

On the previous page the oil demonstration illustrated a monochromatic toning of the subject before proceeding to use color. Below is shown a direct approach using color at the start. This is a typical on-the-spot method, when time is limited and yet you want to capture the essentials of the subject quickly. The tonal and color relationships are estab-lished at the same time. No attempt is made to cover the entire canvas—just place one color against another in as correct a relationship as possible. What you are actually doing is a shorthand version of the subject. Later, in the studio, you can fill in the unpainted areas and complete the details, as shown in the bottom picture.

Without attempting to cover the entire canvas with paint, a spotting in of the various colors as they relate to each other is sought.

Back in the studio the unpainted areas of the canvas are filled in, using the previously laid color spotting as a guide.

UNDERPAINTING IN OIL

Underpainting is a method best accomplished in the quiet of your studio. It entails much planning in the preliminary stage for textural quality and color to be attained in the final painting. A color sketch of the subject should be on hand to refer to during the entire painting.

The following demonstration illustrates one method of using an underpainting, stressing the textural effects. On page 57, the demonstration concentrates on the color effects possible through underpainting.

The staining of the canvas (actually an imprimatura method described on page 61) allows you to see clearly the underpainting white textural lay-in. This step can be dispensed with if your underpainting is done in neutral tints, for the latter contrast sufficiently with the white background of the canvas.

There are fast drying paints made expressly for underpainting. They also accelerate the drying of regular oil colors. I use *M. G. Quick Drying Titanium White*. It spreads evenly, is permanent, and does not crack. It is workable when used directly from the tube and can be thinned with turpentine. The average drying time is from two to four hours. You can then proceed to work in full color.

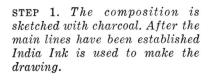

STEP 1. *The composition is sketched with charcoal. After the main lines have been established India Ink is used to make the drawing.*

STEP 2. *A mixture of Raw Umber and Cobalt Blue provide a neutral gray tone that is cut to a watery consistency with copal varnish. It is then applied with a soft, sable brush over the dry inked surface. When the varnish is dry to the touch you can take the next step.*

(continued on next page)

STEP 3. *Using a palette knife, M. G. White is spread over the areas selected to give an interesting textural surface to the subsequent painting. It can be applied in as heavy an impasto manner as desired.*

STEP 4. *Allow from 2 to 4 hours for the underpainting white to dry thoroughly. Now proceed to mix a glaze of one part dammar varnish and five parts of turpentine. This glaze is used as a medium to be mixed with your oil colors. It will make them transparent or semiopaque. depending on the amount of glazing medium used. The illustration on the left shows the lay-in of the glazed colors. In some areas the glaze was omitted and color applied full strength, depending on the effect desired.*

STEP 5. *The painting is resumed, with less glazing, and with more direct handling of the color. Gradually the various areas are refined where necessary, and details added. Some carefully placed accents complete the painting.*

OBTAINING TEXTURAL QUALITY
BY UNDERPAINTING

In this section we will deal with how the surface color can be influenced by underpainting.

The final color effect must be kept in mind when commencing an underpainting. For example, an underpainting can be made in contrasting colors—a blue sky can be underpainted with a light red or orange, a blue undertone can be given to a brown tree trunk, etc.

Or again, the entire underpainting can be done in pale neutral colors and the final color achieved through a series of glazes intensifying the underpainted colors.

It is necessary to use fast-drying colors with heavy body and little oil. While Flake White has for years been used because of its fast-drying properties, the manufacturers of artists' colors are now making a special underpainting white. In the previous section I mentioned the use of *M. G. White*. By mixing this white with your regular oil colors the entire underpainting drying time is greatly accelerated. However, having to use white with all your colors may limit the intensity of the mixture. If you should want to retain all of the saturating qualities of a color, there is a medium on the market called *M. G. Zec*. It is a clear, colorless medium that, when mixed with your regular colors, will speed the drying. It will allow impasto effects, can be thinned with turpentine, and is permanent.

The demonstration on the right illustrates the underpainting procedure with contrasting colors. In the final painting both glazing and impasto techniques were employed.

WORKING WITH TRANSPARENT OIL PAINT

Doing a detailed subject in watercolor has already been described on page 24. You may, nevertheless, have the desire sometime to do a similar subject in oil paint. Ordinarily it is difficult to handle sharp details with this heavier medium, but it is possible through the following method.

The subject is sketched on a smooth canvas or board and then inked in with a fine sable brush. Arrange your regular oil colors on your palette. Instead of using your usual mixing medium, use a preparation known as *Gel*. It cuts the consistency of the oil paint, making the color transparent. Then, prefer-

ably using soft-haired flat sable brushes, proceed to paint over the inked drawing. The latter will show through, allowing the most minute details to remain visible upon completion of the painting.

This is actually a glazing process, commonly done with a mixture of one part stand oil, one part dammar varnish, and five parts turpentine. It is mixed with the oil color and reduced to an almost water-thin consistency. The advantage of *Gel* is that it will reduce the colors equally as well but its jelly-like quality allows you to retain the character of your brush strokes if you so desire.

The top panel, above, shows the color used full strength, with Gel *employed for vigorous brush work. The second panel shows the color gradually cut to the most transparent consistency with* Gel.

At left is shown the inked drawing made preparatory to the application of the transparent oil color. The surface quality is naturally thin in the final painting. To vary the surface, some textural quality can be imparted by carefully manipulating heavier paint to parts of the final painting.

PAINTING OVER A TONED GROUND

Rather than working over the regular canvas, you may want to experiment with a toned surface. You will discover that toning is a time saver when you wish to complete the painting in one sitting.

A toned ground is prepared well in advance, so that it is thoroughly dry when you paint your subject. The usual stretched white canvas or canvas board is used to receive the toned ground. Mix a neutral color, using your usual oil paints. Raw Umber and French Ultramarine with White make an excellent neutral gray tone. A white lead or Flake White is preferable to the customary white paint on your palette. Use copal varnish to thin the paint and with a brush or palette knife (the latter is better) apply the mixture to the canvas. Allow to dry thoroughly—at least a week—and it is ready for use.

You may want to prepare several toned canvases at one time for future work. The toning color can be varied, as well as the intensity of the tone. A warm brown tone, a pale ochre tint or a grayish-green tone are typical colors for such grounds.

The first illustration on the right shows a neutral bluish-gray toned canvas. The composition is then sketched in with charcoal. The surplus charcoal is dusted off and the subject is indicated roughly, using strokes of a neutral color, darker than the toned ground. The latter is approximately the middle tone, so all the darker areas are quickly painted in and keyed to this tone. Use full color, matching as closely as possible the scene before you. The second illustration shows the canvas at the completion of this stage. Note that, so far, no colors that are lighter than the toned ground have been used.

The third illustration shows the final stage. The light areas are painted, wherever possible, and the toned ground is allowed to remain to indicate the middle tone. Incidentally, the toned area that represented the sky seemed to be effective both in color and value, so it was left untouched. Sharp accents were added and the painting was complete.

THE USE OF THE IMPRIMATURA IN OIL PAINTING

A transparent oil glaze or stain is known as the imprimatura. It can be applied at *any stage* of the painting, over the entire canvas or in any particular area. Frequently applied to the white canvas, its purpose is to enhance the subsequent colors.

The imprimatura can be any color. The color selected is cut to a watery consistency with copal varnish. The canvas should be in a horizontal position to prevent running when the stain is applied. When the latter is dry to the touch the painting can begin.

In the demonstration below the yellow imprimatura was applied after the monochromatic lay-in was painted and thoroughly dry.

It could have been done directly on the white canvas, but the effect I wanted to achieve required the warm yellow to dominate the cool blue. When the imprimatura was dry I proceeded to use color, covering those areas shown in the third plate. The painting continued until complete, as shown in the last picture.

I used a flat yellow imprimatura for this demonstration, but you can vary the tonal quality, graduating from light to dark. You can also vary the color, blending two or more colors together. Just remember that the surface to which you apply the glaze must be dry.

THE IMPRIMATURA IN WATERCOLOR

Although used mainly with oil, imprimatura can be effective with watercolor.

Below are two demonstrations showing how the color of the preliminary wash acts as a stain, effecting the subsequent color washes. A unified color harmony results. Care must be taken during the application of color that the preliminary wash is not disturbed. If it is, it mixes with the overlaying color and causes a muddy look. Note that the imprimatura does not necessarily cover the entire paper.

GOUACHE PAINTING

The simplest description of gouache painting is that it is opaque watercolor. There are regular gouache colors manufactured, along with various opaque colors such as poster or showcard colors, tempera, designers colors, and casein paint. They have two points in common—all are soluble in water and all are fast-drying. Transparent watercolor mixed with an opaque color such as Chinese White, becomes a gouache also.

While gouache lacks the fresh transparency achieved with pure watercolor, you will find it easier to handle. Changes and corrections can be made readily, and textures can be obtained that are similar to those of oil paint. Its opaque quality makes it workable on toned paper and many interesting effects can be had on such a base.

Watercolor paper and illustration board are excellent surfaces and your watercolor brushes can be used for general gouache painting. Bristle brushes designed for oil paint are handy for more vigorous techniques and for washing out unwanted areas. (Such brushes should be reserved only for your gouache work.)

The illustration to the left, below, has been overworked—so much so that I was ready to discard it. I thought it might be interesting to experiment with gouache, as a corrective device, over it. I repainted the light areas and unified the color passages in the darks. The final result is shown to the right.

Gouache paintings can be framed like

Top left: gouache paint can be diluted with water similar to a transparent watercolor wash. Top right: with less water, the characteristic opaque effect of gouache. Lower left: gouache has been applied with a stiff bristle brush, resulting in strokes similar to oil paint. In the final illustration, the gouache is applied in a pouncing manner, useful for obtaining textural effects.

watercolors, with the usual glass covering the paintings. Being a heavier medium, they can also be effectively presented in a narrow mat and a wide frame. (See the chapter on Picture Presentation.)

DEMONSTRATION
WITH GOUACHE
ON A TONED PAPER

STEP 1. *A pencil drawing is made of the subject, using a gray paper.*

STEP 2. *The drawing is now intensified with brush and India Ink. The dark areas are brushed in solidly. In the next step, when the color is applied, this ink base will be an important factor in influencing the effect of color.*

STEP 3. *The color in the light areas is applied heavily, completely covering the gray surfaces. However, by adding to the amount of water, passages of color can be diluted, allowing some of the black drawing to show through. Interesting effects can be produced through this method. Also, wherever possible, allow the gray paper to act as a halftone. In the finished painting, the hill in the immediate foreground is almost entirely the original gray paper.*

CASEIN—THE MOST VERSATILE PAINTING MEDIUM

When you consider that a single medium, casein, allows you to work in such a variety of styles—watercolor, gouache, and in an impasto manner—and that, when varnished, it resembles an oil painting, and is excellent for underpainting as well, its importance is apparent. All this plus the fact that casein requires no reorientation in color mixing. All of the principal colors that you use in your watercolor or oil palette are available in casein.

Diluted with water and applied to paper, it dries quickly and resembles a watercolor. With less water and brushed on in a heavier manner, it becomes a gouache. The gouache, when covered with a casein varnish and framed without a mat, takes on the visual effect of an oil painting.

When used as an underpainting for oil, casein dries rapidly. It is then varnished and, when dry to the touch, oil glazes can be applied.

Below is a step-by-step demonstration of casein used as a straight gouache. I find that a heavy handmade watercolor paper or board is best for casein paint. However, any absorbent surface is suitable.

The casein underpainting and the com-

pleted painting with oil glazes are shown here. I first sketched the subject in charcoal on a gesso board. When satisfactory, the surplus was dusted off, leaving a faint image as a guide. I then applied the casein paint. Care was exercised in the painting of the color areas, for I kept in mind the effect of the oil glazes that were to follow. If the casein should dry too quickly and make the brush handling difficult, you can use a casein painting medium that acts as a retarder. Use it with water, in the proportions varying from one to three parts emulsion to five parts of water.

STEP 1. *Using a gesso board, the subject is sketched in lightly with charcoal. Dusting off the surplus charcoal, the faint image remaining serves as a guide for a redrawing of the subject, using a Cobalt Blue casein color. This is followed by the painting of the various objects in rather subdued casein colors. It is preferable that the casein lay-in be restrained, keeping in mind that the full color saturation will be achieved with subsequent oil color glazes. The completed casein lay-in is shown here.*

STEP 2. *The casein lay-in is then covered with a varnish made expressly for isolating the casein paint from the oil glazes which are to follow. The varnish dries quickly. It will be immediately noted that the varnish intensifies the casein color. This is another reason why the original lay-in should be on the light and subdued side. The glazes for the oil color can be made as previously described in "Underpainting." It is best that the full saturation of the oil glazes not be accomplished at the first application, but rather through a series of glazes. Greater luminosity is achieved this way. Remember to use soft-haired sable brushes so that the glazes are applied in an even manner. As you work with oil color you may be able to attain more textural quality in certain areas by applying the paint solidly, instead of glazing. Upon completion, the subject is considered an oil painting and framed accordingly. It can be given a coat of the regular final oil painting varnish after three to six months.*

RENDERING WITH CHARCOAL

Although charcoal is generally thought of in terms of making life-drawing studies, it can be combined very well with watercolor.

The subject can be done on charcoal paper, but watercolor paper, with a surface rough enough to hold the charcoal, will take the subsequent color washes much better. Make the drawing directly with charcoal from the start. Work lightly, gradually working into the dark areas and keeping your strokes clean and crisp. Avoid rubbing, as the broken stroke produced by direct handling allows the white of the paper to show through. This is essential in order to obtain luminosity when the color washes are applied over the charcoal. This is particularly true when doing the dark areas in order to avoid muddy effects. When the charcoal drawing is completed, spray it with fixative.

The color washes should be mixed in a bright, high key, as the charcoal undertone will lower the visual effect of the color.

Interesting effects can also be obtained by not fixing the charcoal. When working in this manner, avoid as many black areas as possible. Instead, keep the entire drawing fairly light in your initial attempts. The watercolor must be deftly applied, for the color mixes immediately with the charcoal. Use as large a brush as possible. This method is most effective when soft edges are desired.

In either method, it is possible to go back to the charcoal once the watercolor is dry. This may be necessary in order to make some sharp accents or more modeling. The disadvantage of doing additional charcoal work is in the difficulty of spraying it with fixative without affecting the watercolor.

I have found charcoal an ideal medium for making monochromatic tonal studies preparatory to painting.

Reproduced below is the study for the painting, "Joe's Lunch." I accomplished most of the work with soft charcoal on gray paper. Then the white of the light striking the snow was put in with white casein. The completed study gave me a fairly good idea of the arrangement of the values before I started to work on the actual painting.

"Joe's Lunch" — Collection Syracuse University

66

USING A CHARCOAL
BASE FOR WATERCOLOR

STEP 1. *The main lines of the composition are indicated in charcoal on a rough watercolor board.*

STEP 2. *The charcoal is applied in a direct manner. Avoid rubbing and keep the strokes clean and crisp, allowing the white surface to come through. A rough watercolor board helps to accomplish this, as the raised textured surface readily breaks through the charcoal.*

STEP 3. *The charcoal drawing is sprayed with fixative to prevent smudging or smearing when the watercolor washes are applied. The painting is started by covering the large areas first. In this subject I painted the outer walls first and gradually worked back into the yard. It may be necessary to use some touches of opaque color as the painting nears completion, particularly when the charcoal underdrawing is too heavy.*

CHARCOAL BASE FOR COLOR WASHES

The vignettes below have all been made with charcoal on a rough watercolor paper. They were then sprayed with fixative. The watercolor washes were applied in as direct a manner as possible, allowing the charcoal base to carry the modeling. Some touches of opaque watercolor were used to spark a dull passage, or to produce a sharp accent.

Colored inks can be substituted for watercolor. They are composed of aniline dyes and will show up more vividly over the charcoal. Compared to colored inks, the pigment in watercolor has a tendency to lower the transparent quality.

PEN AND INK FOUNDATION FOR WATERCOLOR

In the pages that follow, various methods of employing pen and ink with watercolor are described. A simple but effective combination is demonstrated here.

I made a pencil drawing of the subject on watercolor paper. I followed with an inking-in, using India Ink. As the latter is waterproof, there is no danger of it running into the subsequent watercolor washes.

In rendering the ink drawing, I tried to avoid the obvious use of pen lines. I wanted the black ink to serve as a foundation for the watercolor, but not to dominate the final painting. I massed the darks whenever possible and suggested only a minimum amount of texture in the light areas. Occasionally the paper was moistened with clear water so that a blurred, rather than a sharp black line resulted.

The covering of the ink foundation with watercolor washes is shown in the second illustration. An imprimatura method was partly employed, particularly in the sky area. Note the preliminary warm wash of Umber that was put over this area.

In the final stage, I applied the color washes in full strength. The blue sky has attained more luminosity and color quality through the imprimatura painting.

While the ink foundation is still apparent in the finished painting, it is subordinate to the watercolor washes. You may want to experiment with other colored inks as a foundation. Any color can be used, or it can be mixed with the India Ink. Just make certain that it is waterproof.

69

COLORED INKS

Colored inks have been frowned upon by the purists, as some colors are fugitive and, after a period of time, will begin to fade.

However, colored inks have many advantages. They are transparent, and several coats of color can be applied over a single area. The full transparency is still retained, as the underlaying color adheres firmly to the paper and does not mix with the overlaying color as in watercolor. Care should be taken not to apply the preliminary ink wash too heavily, but to dilute it well with water. Colored inks have a strong staining power and are difficult to tone down once they are put on paper. They are also waterproof; it is this quality that allows you to superimpose as many washes as needed to obtain the depth of color desired.

I once had occasion to visit the *Famous Artists School* in Westport, Connecticut as a guest of its distinguished president, Albert Dorne. Being an admirer of Dorne's work for years, I inquired about his illustrations that were hanging on the office walls. They possessed such a beautiful depth of rich color that I took them for oil paintings, yet they had a luminosity generally attained only with watercolor. I was very much surprised when Dorne said that they were painted with colored inks. Some of them were several years old, but none of the color passages revealed any signs of fading. Dorne told me that he put a coat of clear varnish over them, made up of pure dammar varnish and pure spirits of turpentine in equal parts. He also revealed that he underpaints with black waterproof ink and then applies the colored inks as glazes.

There is no doubt that this is an excellent method of keeping the subject under control from start to finish—particularly for so fine an artist as Albert Dorne!

Below are shown some of the textures that can be obtained with ink. They are particularly useful when preparing an undertone for subsequent color washes. All were done on a surface that was first moistened with clear water. Then, using a pen, black ink was applied. In some cases brown ink was added and allowed to intermingle with the black ink. Scratching out of textures was accomplished with a razor blade.

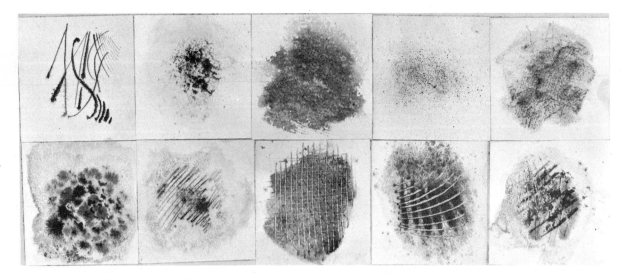

INK UNDERTONE FOR WATERCOLOR

An ink undertone can, to a degree, be likened to an underpainting for oil color. It carries the drawing and tentatively defines the form and tonal relationships. It also influences the final color effect, depending upon the amount of colored inks used in the undertone. The two plates on the bottom of the following page illustrate the latter point.

It might be wise to limit your initial experimenting to a single-color ink undertone.

Directly below, a black ink undertone is shown. I have attempted to break away, through various devices, from any conventional pen-and-ink technique. First, I wet the paper with clear water to avoid hard pen lines. At times the water was applied freely, at other times the paper was just slightly dampened. This varying of the surface moisture affected the ink lines. Again, I resorted to the brush to create halftones where necessary. When the paper was dry, fine pen lines were used for details and accents. I waited for the latter to dry before applying watercolor washes.

On page 69, the penwork of the ink drawing for the demonstration was retained in the final painting. In this method the ink undertone has a wash quality. As the watercolor is applied, the ink undertone gradually blends with the overlaying color washes.

The finished watercolor painting is shown here. Note how the ink undertone influences the form and tonal relationship of the subject, yet blends harmoniously with overlaying washes of watercolor.

COLORED INK DEMONSTRATIONS

Here the subject is rendered, using a straight pen-and-ink technique. A moist surface has been employed to vary the pen lines. Brown waterproof ink was used. Then, using colored inks diluted with water, the painting began. Care must be exercised in applying the ink washes so that they are not too strong and do not stain the paper too deeply at the start.

The Ink Undertone

On the previous page the ink undertone was painted in a single color. Here we see two colors employed—Brown and Neutral Tint—with the former dominating the color combinations. The entire drawing and the tonal values are rendered before proceeding with watercolor.

The Watercolor is Applied

The watercolor washes can be applied as soon as the ink undertone is dry. Dilute the colors well for they should be as transparent as possible to allow the ink undertone to provide the modeling. Keep in mind that watercolor paints vary in degrees of opacity,

INK COMBINED WITH WATERCOLOR

It is difficult to surpass the combination of ink and watercolor when a sharp, accurate delineation of the subject is required.

Directly below is a reproduction of a subject painted with watercolor. It certainly shows the location of the plant and the surrounding terrain accurately enough. However, in order to show all of the building details, a very tight, hard watercolor of the center of interest would have to be made. Then the surrounding terrain would have to be done in a similar style so that the building would not look foreign to the background. In all, it would have resulted in an architectural rendering rather than a painting.

A happy compromise is to use watercolor in as direct and freely handled manner as desired. Then, using pen and ink (brown in this picture) render the necessary details. The pen work would be carried throughout the rest of the picture to achieve a harmonious over-all effect.

It is not necessary to start with watercolor. You may want to do the pen-and-ink work first, or at least part of it, depicting the general drawing. Then apply the color and finish the final details with the pen. Personally, I find it best only to suggest the composition with pen and go into color as soon as possible.

The watercolor painting of the subject.

The combination watercolor and pen drawing of the subject.

73

PEN AND WASH DRAWING

Pen and wash drawings and tinted monochromes preceded watercolor painting as we know it today.

As far back as the Renaissance, artists used the combination of pen and wash. At the end of the 18th Century, the English artist, William Payne, experimented with eliminating the drawn outline. The outline had served in creating boundaries that limited color washes to areas restricted by line.

When something is old and therefore respectable enough to become classical, it becomes fashionable to revive it. Illustrators make frequent use of this ancient technique to create atmospheric effects in assignments dealing with the past.

Variations on this technique also appear from time to time in watercolor exhibitions. They may range from the conservative retaining of the entire pen outline to the modern calligraphic line.

The pen drawing is made with a heavy stub pen.

A watercolor black is diluted with water and the tonal washes are applied.

74

PEN AND INK OUTLINE FOR WATERCOLOR PAINTING

In the previous chapters, whenever pen and ink were combined with watercolor the pen work helped create the textures for the final painting.

Another approach to combining the two mediums is to employ the pen to make an outline only for the subject. By doing the outline first the drawing of the subject is crystalized at the start. You are then free to concentrate on the watercolor. This method is shown in the top illustration.

A variation of this method is to reverse the process—do the watercolor first and then outline the painted areas with a pen. The second illustration demonstrates this approach. While it is difficult to distinguish which procedure was used in the final picture, each method has its advantages.

When the watercolor is painted first the outlining can be done more selectively. That is, you use lines only where they are needed to separate one object or area from another, thus producing an over-all effect of greater clarity. By shortening the lines and using a flexible pen point, a calligraphic effect can be achieved which will impart much verve to the subject. The subjects below were sketched directly with the pen, omitting the usual preliminary penciling. This is an excellent exercise in training the eye to observe before any lines are applied to the paper.

Unlike penciled lines, which can easily be erased and redrawn, the ink line is an immediate commitment.

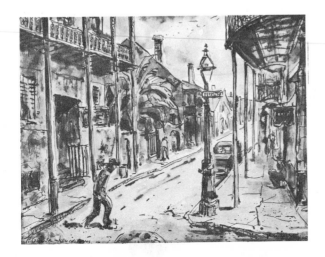

DEVELOPING A PEN DRAWING INTO A WATERCOLOR

The following demonstration shows how the pictorial conception has been developed into a pen and ink watercolor. While the drawing is, in itself, a complete black and white rendering of the subject, it can be carried on in color. Below is a pen drawing

STEP 1. *The main lines of the composition are roughly indicated in pencil.*

STEP 2. *This is followed by the inking in of the subject. In this demonstration India Ink has been used. The pen lines follow the contours of the various shapes whenever possible. The completed pen drawing is shown here.*

76

showing the initial application of watercolor washes and the completed painting. In this instance, no attempt was made to keep all of the washes transparent. Where necessary to add color or textural impact, the pen work was partially or totally obliterated.

STEP 3. *The watercolor painting starts by covering the various areas with light washes of their approximate color. The pen lines still dominate the subject. Then, starting with the sky, fully saturated color washes are applied. The sky is completed at this stage.*

STEP 4. *The increasingly strong color washes are continued and, in the same areas, the pen work is almost obliterated. However, at the completion of the painting enough of the lines show through to help convey a feeling of solidity and texture to the watercolor.*

USING THE PEN TO ACCENT A WATERCOLOR

This is a method of using pen and ink as a means of accenting and adding textural effects at the final stage of a watercolor, or of any painting in a water soluble medium.

The painting reproduced below was done with some passages in casein to impart textural effects. The painting still seemed to lack emphasis—it appeared to have an undesirable flatness.

Using a crow-quill point with black ink, I proceeded to accent the dark areas which were at right angles to the light areas. This perked up the painting a bit, so I continued using the pen. Some of the objects were partially outlined and sharp accents were put in. The latter helped, particularly in the shaded areas, to make the shadows look more transparent. A weather-beaten look was immediately imparted to the roof of the barn with a few crisp strokes. The pen work was concluded with the sharpening of the trees.

The flexible point of the crow-quill pen was most effective in rendering the branches as they tapered away from the trunk.

You do not have to restrict the color of the ink just to black. Brown ink as well as the several other colors that are manufactured may be used. Again, you may want to use different colors on the same painting. Warm colors can be used in the foreground objects and cooler ones as the objects recede.

In a later chapter the use of the brush is described as a means of strengthening areas in a painting. The same can be accomplished with pen and ink. By judicious pen work you can often strengthen the outline of objects that are weak in values or in relation to each other. Heavy lines will bring the object forward and thin lines will cause it to recede.

While I have recommended the crow-quill pen as being of value because of its flexibility, you may want to experiment with other pen points. A speed-ball point, for example, will give you a heavy unwavering line.

FOUNTAIN PEN

Of all the portable drawing aids available to the artist, the fountain pen is invaluable when small, sharply delineated line sketches are desired. While the fountain pen can be used on all types of surfaces, a smooth, hard paper will give the best results. With a pad of such paper and a fountain pen, you have all the equipment needed to produce a wealth of sketches.

While I prefer to use a finely pointed pen, a variety of nibs are available. Choose a pen with a nib that produces a line best suited to the particular technique you will use for general sketching. A fine point is excellent for making intimate sketches, along with small notations that are clearly legible for later reference.

A stub point will be found useful for broader effects and can render a more flexible line than the fine point. The ball-point pen has become increasingly popular with artists who are interested in producing an unwavering, stylized line of even thickness.

The color and even the permanency of the ink is controlled by the type of pen you use. Since the fountain pen is designed primarily for writing, the available inks are generally blue or blue-black. These inks are considered semipermanent or moderately permanent. The lines produced will remain legible indefinitely, but the color hue will weaken. The line of the ball-point pen is the least perm-

anent, but improvements are rapidly being made in the color formula.

There are especially designed fountain pens made to hold the regular jet-black India drawing ink, they are expensive and care must be taken to keep them workable.

The sketch in the upper right corner was made with a fine-point fountain pen and is reproduced about half size.

At the bottom of the page are shown sketches that are really "shorthand" notes. I use them as an aid for future use in identifying color effects from a photograph of the

subject. Such notes generally are done when I am on a trip. Although I may be pressed for time, if I see something of interest I make a photographic record of it along with these quick notes.

The illustrations on this page show two different techniques that can be obtained with the same fountain pen. On the right is a "scribble" technique—an approach used to suggest tonal values rather than the usual line interpretation of a subject. This is an excellent way of relieving any tightness you may have acquired by being too concerned with a finished technical effect.

The illustration below is an opposite approach—here the problem is one of making disciplined studies directly from nature. Your principal concern is in getting as much anatomical detail as possible. This type of rendering serves two purposes. First, it is an exercise in disciplined drawing, and helps you avoid a careless interpretation. Second, it is a means of acquiring detailed material for future studio painting reference.

BRUSH DRAWING

I have previously mentioned certain brushes useful for lay-in work, underpainting, glazing, etc. You will find the red sable watercolor brush to be the most useful for brush drawing. There are about 15 sizes available, from a triple zero, which renders as finely as a pen, to extra large architectural rendering brushes. The large brushes are generally used for watercolor painting. For the average brush drawing, a number four is a popular size. A small bristle brush is handy for varying the textural effect.

How you handle the brush vitally affects the stroke. Grasping it by the ferrule will enable you to control the placing of details or sharp details. For general work, broader handling is attained by holding the brush closer to the center of the handle. As you work you may even hold it near the tip for greater freedom. Interesting strokes can be made by twirling the brush between your forefinger and thumb. This produces a broken and softer line in contrast to the result obtained when the brush is gripped by the ferrule. I suggest that you practice various brush strokes. Note that at the start of a stroke, the line is heavier and tapers as the brush goes away from you. Make strokes from the left to the right and vice-versa, and practice vertical strokes. All this will help in acquiring facility with the brush and will leave you free to concentrate on the more important aspects of picture making.

When you dip your brush into the color or ink, the amount of liquid gathered by the brush will affect the stroke. This is most vital when doing a dry-brush rendering as described on page 87. Another factor to consider is the surface of the paper used. The brush stroke glides over smooth paper compared to the resistance encountered when using rough paper. Rinse your brush thoroughly right after you use it. Squeeze out the surplus water by placing the brush between the thumb and index finger, reshaping the hairs to a point. Ink is best removed by washing the brush with soap and lukewarm water. Again rinse thoroughly with clear water to remove all of the soap, and repeat the shaping process.

Both of these watercolors were done directly with the brush, omitting the preliminary pencil planning. Popularly known as "quickies," these are done rapidly, and generally worked on a quarter-size sheet of paper—roughly 11 x 14 inches. This is an excellent way to record transient moods with spontaneous brushwork.

BRUSH DRAWING FOR PLANNING COMPOSITIONS

I find the sable brush a most sympathetic implement when planning rough compositions in which I want to establish the dark pattern quickly. Using black drawing ink and a fairly smooth paper, I make several thumbnail arrangements. Working in a small size at first and at times in an semiabstract style, I gradually increase the size of the composition. I work more realistically as the size increases. Then, on arriving at one that has painting possibilities, I redraw it on canvas or watercolor paper—depending upon the painting medium I intend to use.

If I need a model I do not use one until I have established the composition. Then I make separate drawings in charcoal or pencil and use them as reference when redrawing the composition for the final painting.

Rough brush drawings are also helpful in planning landscape compositions. Preliminary vertical and horizontal arrangements of the subject below were made before the composition was selected for the final painting.

"The Querril's Place" — Collection Newark Museum

BRUSH AND INK BASE FOR COLOR OVERPAINTING

On the previous page, brush and ink were used for the preliminary compositions only. In this section and the demonstrations that follow, brush and ink are part of the painted picture.

On the right is shown a brush drawing on a gray tinted paper. The ink has been diluted so that halftone areas could be indicated. For the darks, the ink was used full strength. The ink dries quickly, so you can use color almost immediately. As the ink base has been planned to control the final effect through the use of transparent and opaque color, casein paints are used.

Employing the casein in a transparent manner, flat color washes are applied over the inked halftone areas. As you paint you will note how the inked undertone both models and neutralizes the color. Use less water as you approach the dark areas. This will add more covering power to the color but not enough to kill the blacks. However, enough color will remain on these dark areas so that an over-all harmonious effect can be achieved. Where it is necessary to add stronger color passages within the dark areas, use the casein full strength so that it becomes opaque. You will also have to paint the extreme lights in the same manner. This method is a good one for producing low-keyed subjects.

On the following page the demonstration illustrates the use of a brush and black ink base, using only transparent watercolor to achieve the final color effect. Here the brush drawing remains visible in the finished painting. The ink is applied on a white paper, for the later color washes should be as luminous as possible. It is this luminosity, with the black drawing acting as a foil, that makes the final results most effective.

On page 85, the demonstration shown is a combination of the two previously described. The usual ink drawing is made and transparent opaque washes of casein are used for color. Wherever possible the black ink base is allowed to remain to carry the drawing.

For example, the color areas are painted around the black outlines. This can be noted in the foreground where the dark outlines accent the various figures and objects. Then, as the figures and objects recede, the outline is blurred or completely eliminated. This method is particularly adaptable for busy subjects depicting several figures and objects. The retaining of the outline emphasizes the portions you want to emphasize. The blurring, followed by elimination of the line entirely, subdues those that are secondary.

BRUSH AND INK FOUNDATION FOR GOUACHE

STEP 1. *A pencil drawing is made, depicting the main lines of the subject.*

STEP 2. *This is followed by a brush drawing, using India Ink. The shadows and heavy masses are brushed in, allowing bits of the white paper to show through to avoid a heavy, dull effect.*

STEP 3. *Working from light to dark, the watercolor washes are applied. This method is particularly effective when doing subjects containing strong light and dark masses.*

BRUSH AND INK
FOUNDATION
FOR WATERCOLOR

STEP 1. *The usual pencil drawing is made indicating the general composition of the buildings and the placing of the various figures.*

STEP 2. *Using brush and ink, the main lines and masses of the subject are depicted. The brush drawing can be done in a bold manner. The subsequent painting will be opaque enough to thin or reduce any lines that may appear too heavy.*

STEP 3. *Enough water is used with the gouache to make it workable. The color is applied in an oil painting manner, occasionally varying the surfaces of some of the areas by adding more water. As the painting nears completion it may be desirable to restore or add some black outlines. Use black gouache paint rather than the ink. There is always the possibility of the latter flaking off a painted surface.*

USING A BRUSH OUTLINE TO STRENGTHEN A WEAK PAINTING

All of us make our share of paintings that do not turn out as we had planned. This is true more of watercolors than of oil paintings, since the former depend upon a direct, fresh approach in handling the drawing, color, and values—frequently in a single operation. Oils, on the other hand, can be worked over until the corrections are made.

A watercolor that is weak in values and in the delineation of the elements that make up the composition, can frequently be strengthened by outlining the various objects.

The illustrations below show a "before-and-after" treatment of the outline method.

Weak values contribute to the anemic, pale look of this watercolor. As a result, the various forms appear lost.

The watercolor has now been strengthened by the simple operation of outlining, and in some instances massing the shaded areas. A sepia color was used in this painting. However, any deep color that was harmonious to the subject could have been used.

DRY-BRUSH

Dry-brush is a method of obtaining broken strokes that impart an interesting textural effect to a black and white drawing. A minimum amount of ink is used on the brush, which, when applied over a rough paper, deposits the ink in a series of tones varying from gray to black. The gray tones are produced by a light touch and by wiping the surplus ink on a piece of scrap paper before making the stroke. You can obtain a darker effect by increasing the pressure on the brush as well as by adding more ink.

The dry-brush method can also be used with watercolor. The paint is applied with just enough water to transfer the pigment to the paper. It imparts a vitality and an interesting textural quality to the subject.

Old brushes, especially soft sables that no longer come to a point, are excellent for dry-brush technique. Bristle brushes can also be used, although they are better when working large.

On the right is a dry-brush drawing of the quarry subject that served as a guide for the watercolor reproduced below. The drawing,

approximately 9 x 12 inches, was executed on an area large enough to work, using a dry-brush technique. At the same time it was small enough to cover the area in a single session. This is an important consideration as dry-brush rendering is not a fast technique.

The painting was made in the studio. I used watercolor in a dry-brush manner wherever the textures, suggested by the drawing, were applicable.

DRY-BRUSH INK BASE WITH WATERCOLOR

A dry-brush ink base may be likened to a pen-and-ink foundation in that the monochromatic rendering establishes the drawing for the application of color that follows.

Take care not to let the dark areas become too solid; allow bits of the white paper to come through so that the subsequent color will show up. You will thus avoid the deadening effect of solid black. This is particularly true in the shaded areas where a transparent quality is needed in the shadows.

I suggest that you make a careful pencil drawing so that you will know just where the light and dark areas are to be inked in. Caution is important, because any erasing that might be needed to remove unwanted ink areas will affect the surface of the paper and possibly cause the watercolor to lie unevenly.

In the following section the ink base is omitted. Instead, all of the dry-brush effects are accomplished with watercolor.

STEP 1. *A careful pencil drawing is made of the subject. A rough-textured watercolor paper is used.*

STEP 2. *Using a No. 4 pointed sable brush, the subject is inked in. The blacks are kept to a minimum, since the subsequent watercolor washes will take care of the shaded areas.*

A same-size section of the dry-brush drawing is shown above. Note that the blacks have not been put in solidly. The white paper has deliberately been allowed to break through. This will add luminosity to the final watercolor painting.

STEP 3. *Watercolor washes are now applied, working from light to dark. In some areas, notably the shaded parts, warm and cool washes were alternated, thus adding a vibrant quality to the final painting.*

DRY-BRUSH WITH PURE WATERCOLOR

The same approach used when working in the dry-brush technique with ink, is followed with watercolor. Just enough water is used to transfer the paint to the paper. You do not need to do the entire painting, however, in a dry-brush manner. Actually, a more pleasing visual effect is achieved by combining this dry method with some areas that are painted in a fluid method. You will note that in the demonstration, the big areas are given a preliminary flat wash of color before the dry-brush technique is used. The general color scheme is then quickly arrived at through these flat color washes. Dry-brush allows areas of underpainting to show through and imparts a textural effect to a watercolor. It is also an easier way of controlling the modeling of the various forms.

STEP 1. *Using a rough watercolor paper, a pencil drawing is made of the subject. The cast shadows are indicated.*

STEP 2. *The sky is painted in a fluid manner, followed by the hills and trees. Then, reducing the amount of water used, the middle distance is painted in a semidry-brush technique. Note how the rough areas of the white paper break through the color. The rough texture of the road is indicated, with just enough water to make the paint workable.*

STEP 3. *Returning to the fluid style, the barns and foreground area are given a flat wash of color. When these areas are dry a preparatory color wash is painted over the large tree and fence posts in the foreground.*

STEP 4. *Now the shaded areas of the barns are painted, along with their cast shadows. This is followed by painting the bare trees in the upper right area, and the cast shadows in the foreground. At the conclusion of this step the dry-brush technique is resumed, starting with the foliage at the base of the picture.*

STEP 5. *From now to the finish of the painting, only the dry-brush technique is used. Many interesting effects can be obtained by dragging the side, or heel, of the brush over the rough paper. I suggest that you use old brushes for such work. This reproduction shows the many areas of the painting where the final dry-brush work has imparted textural effect and more solidity to the various objects.*

91

DRY-BRUSH WITH GOUACHE ON A TONED SURFACE

One of the pleasures of experimenting with mixed media is in achieving a special effect that could not be obtained with a single medium.

I had been observing the demolition of a building. Each time I passed by more of the outer walls had been torn down, and it had reached the stage where the inside rooms were revealed. The striking effect of the warm, bright colors of the interior contrasted greatly with the dull, grayed remains of the weather-beaten walls and surrounding buildings. And to complete the mood it was a gray day with an overcast sky!

I thought that the subject had excellent possibilities and made a sketch. I did some additional detailed drawings, along with penciled color notations.

Back in the studio my problem was how to interpret the subject—what medium would be the most appropriate. It was highly important that the contrast be dramatic.

I had a mounted sheet of gray charcoal paper on hand and began a lightly handled, sort of feeling-my-way drawing approach, with a stick of charcoal. I sketched the general composition and then dusted off the surplus charcoal. With the remaining faint image as a guide, I started to make a dry-brush drawing of the subject with black ink and an old blunted brush.

The subject gradually took form; how it looked at this stage is illustrated below at the left.

Then, using casein paint in a gouache technique, I painted only the inside area that had been so vividly revealed when the outer walls were demolished. Once this area was completed I stopped and wondered about going on with the painting. I had achieved the contrasting effect I wanted—was it necessary to paint the surrounding area in a low key to hold the effect? I decided not to do any more with the subject and had it framed and exhibited. A fellow artist, whose work I admire very much, bought the painting; what better tribute could I ask!

The dry-brush drawing on the toned paper is shown above.

Using casein in a gouache technique, the vital area of the subject is painted as shown at right.

FELT-PEN

The felt-tipped pen is rapidly becoming one of the most popular sketching implements. It is similar to a fountain pen in that it contains a reservoir of ink. It also has the advantages of a brush, for broad, black effects are quickly rendered as well as thin, pencil-like strokes.

There are available four nibs, which produce various effects. Of added value, particularly to the sketcher working outdoors, is that the nibs are easily interchangeable.

The ink is controlled by the pressure applied as the felt tip touches the paper. Care must be taken not to apply too much pressure, otherwise the ink will flow very heavily. It takes a little practice to manipulate different techniques, such as dry-brush and halftone effects.

Experiment with various paper surfaces. You will probably find a textured paper best for all-round sketching.

On the right are two examples of felt pen sketches. The one on the top was made with a square nib, which tends to produce a stylized stroke. The broad side as well as the corner of the nib is utilized.

A small round chisel-tipped nib was used for the other illustration. A thinner, "sketchy" effect can be obtained with this nib.

The one disadvantage of the pen is that the ink that must be used is made of aniline dye with an oil base. While it is waterproof and permanent to the extent that it will not rub off, strong light will cause some fading over a period of time.

"Evening Boatyard" — *Salmagundi Club Black and White Prize*

THE FELT-PEN BASE FOR COLOR

While black and brown are the colors most commonly used in the felt pen, there are several other colors available. However, a separate pen is necessary for each color, and carrying a dozen or so pens is a bit cumbersome! I prefer to use the black or brown ink as a base and if I desire color I apply watercolor washes over the inked sketch. The reproduction on the right is an example of such a procedure. The main lines and some shaded areas were indicated with the felt pen, using brown ink. I then painted over the ink drawing with transparent watercolor.

A Demonstration of Using a Felt Pen Base for Watercolor

STEP 1. *Omitting a pencil drawing, the subject is sketched directly with the felt pen. A brown ink on watercolor paper is used in this demonstration. Only a small portion of the shaded area is indicated, as the main shadows are to be painted with watercolor.*

STEP 2. *The watercolor washes are applied in a free manner, working from light to dark. They are kept transparent so that the felt pen lines will be clearly visible in the final painting. This method is most effective in producing free, sketchy impressions of the subject.*

PENCIL SKETCHING

The fact that I discuss pencil sketching after three-quarters of this book has been devoted to various mediums and methods, should not be interpreted to mean that I think pencil sketching is unimportant. Actually, the pencil has been the one sketching implement vitally necessary from the very start, not only of this book, but of the student's art career as well.

On this page are shown two widely different methods of employing a pencil. On the right are rough thumbnail sketches which illustrate how I gradually crystalized an idea into a composition. These are preliminary scribblings from which the germ of an idea takes form. From such vague sketches the artist hopes to find one of sufficient possibilities to develop into a finished composition. With the variety of pencils available, tones ranging from a hard, light gray to a deep, velvety black can be rendered.

Such drawings are best accomplished on a kid-finish, heavy paper or board. Using a soft pencil with a chiseled point, the drawing is generally rendered with broad strokes, following the contours of the various forms that make up the subject.

PENCIL SKETCHING

Two contrasting examples of the use of a pencil are shown on this page.

The drawing on the right illustrates the use of a pencil in a thin, stylus-like line. This simplified outline drawing is frequently used by the watercolorist as a guide for color washes. Occasionally some textures are suggested, but they are usually kept to a minimum of penciling. Handling the pencil in such a manner is also an excellent exercise for carefully delineated drawing, working directly from nature. The point of the pencil is kept needle-sharp. A hard and sometimes cold line is produced in contrast to the usual searching, feeling-for-the-form soft line, that is generally associated with pencil drawing.

Below are a group of quick pencil sketches. They were made from a train window on a small pad about 3 x 5 inches. It is in the doing of such sketches when time is limited, that the pencil is an unsurpassed tool.

Experiment with the different papers that are available. Mention has already been made of kid-finish paper. It has a surface most sympathetic to the pencil and lends itself readily to correction by eraser. Interesting effects are also obtained with smooth and clay-coated papers. They are particularly adaptable to direct handling, with a minimum use of the eraser. Always keep several

sheets of paper, to act as padding, under the sheet upon which you are working. When the drawing is finished it can be sprayed with fixative or a plastic spray, to prevent smudging.

Because of the many technical methods that are discussed in this book, I have not been able to devote the space required for a medium as important as pencil sketching. I suggest that you obtain Ernest Watson's books on pencil sketching, along with those of Ted Kautzky and Arthur Guptill. They are the outstanding books in their field and should be in every art student's library.

Shown below, a group of pencil sketches made in an afternoon's work gathering material for a studio painting. How such sketches are used is described in the following pages.

WORKING IN THE STUDIO FROM PENCIL NOTES

As the student progresses, he becomes increasingly aware of the importance of his sketch book. Although he may be working on the spot in full color, it is in the sketch book that he has made his compositional notes prior to the painting of the subject. Along with these notes, he lists important supplementary data, including details to be incorporated into the studio painting of the subject. It is in the sketch book that he records the life around him—street scenes, people at work and play, pencil notations of new color schemes, etc.

In the previous section the various pencil techniques have been discussed. In some of the methods the technique described was one that could be an expression complete in itself. Other techniques were recommended for the gathering of notes for future reference.

Such a note is shown on the right. After the subject has been sketched, some indication of the light and shade is depicted. As we are to depend upon the color notations as our chief guide, only a minimum amount of shading is required. When making the color notations it is not necessary to hold to the paint manufacturer's terminology. For example, an object whose local color was a pale

Alizarin Crimson could be noted as just "pinkish."

You might also want to use a device that I have found to be most helpful. Say that an area is a subtle grayish-brown color, with a touch of olive green. It so happens that the walls of my studio possess about the same coloration. I then write "studio walls" over the area. Later, when I am painting the subject, the color association registers immediately. This method of associating the colors in the subject with colors that you come in contact with daily, can be of immense help.

A strong effort has been made to capture an "on-the-spot outdoors" feeling in the studio painting shown here.

You will note that the finished painting on this page was painted in a different proportion than the penciled note.

You will find as you work from pencil notes, that frequently you will rearrange the subject in the final painting. I have found it feasible to include as much subject information as possible in such notes. Then, when I start the sketch for the studio painting, I can use whatever I think necessary. I am free to eliminate areas and tighten up the over-all composition.

The leaf from my sketch book, reproduced below, shows what I mean. By making the sketch of a wider proportion than I generally paint, I am able to include more data. Back in the studio I compose the subject on an almost squarely proportioned canvas. The finished painting is shown at the bottom of the page.

Note that, while the general character of the pencil note has been retained in the studio painting, the proportions of the latter have been drastically changed. Along with an elongation of the houses, the perspective of the receding street has been altered to condense further the subject in the studio interpretation.

THE PENCIL DRAWING AS A TONAL STUDY

In the section on "Pencil Sketching" one of the techniques mentioned was broad stroke.

The broad-stroke technique gives an interpretation of the subject with a full tonal range, from the white of the paper, to the intermediary grays, and then to the deepest of blacks. This tonal drawing is a helpful reference in the studio when doing a painting of the subject. The flat and graded effects of this pencil technique are of particular aid to the watercolorist.

As such drawings are complete renderings in themselves, you undoubtedly are reluctant to make pencil notations of colors over them. Simply make your notations, referring to the color of the various objects and passages, on the margin of the drawing. In this manner the drawing is preserved intact and still serves its purpose for reference.

Note how the watercolor reproduced below has followed the tonal qualities of the pencil drawing on the right.

You will find the broad-stroke pencil technique of immeasureable help in making

supplementary drawings when painting on the spot, for you can concentrate on the color effects that take place. Drawings can then be made of cloud arrangements, tonal details of various objects, etc. All of these can be incorporated into the finished studio painting.

DEMONSTRATION OF WORKING FROM A PENCIL NOTE

It is extremely unlikely that you will always have on hand color media with which to capture a fleeting effect. Even if you should be so equipped, the effect would probably vanish by the time you had everything in readiness. However, the ever present pencil and pad will enable you to make at least a quick note, rough as it may be, for possible future use.

I was walking along a road near the waterfront as it was nearing dusk. The last rays of the sun behind the buildings silhouetted them against a brilliant sky and cloud effect. I quickly made the pencil sketch, with color notations, shown at the right. Later, referring to the sketch, I made the watercolor shown below.

STEP 1. *After the preliminary penciling has been done, the sky, which is the most vital area of the picture, is painted.*

STEP 2. *While the sky is drying, the lights in the houses and foreground area are painted. Then, when these are dry, the big, dark masses follow. The shadow in the immediate foreground has been improvised because I felt that the subject needed a dark base for balance.*

PAINTING DIRECTLY OVER A PENCIL SKETCH

You may wish to experiment by using some of your old pencil sketches as bases for watercolors.

On the right is an industrial subject that was originally rendered in tone with pencil. The watercolor is floated over the sketch, allowing the pencil drawing to show through. The color has been applied, mainly in a flat manner, allowing the penciled toning underneath to do the modeling.

Another method is illustrated below. It is a sketch in outline, with penciled notations

indicating color. This method allows a more direct handling of the color; modeling is achieved through successive washes. The original color notations can be followed and then removed with a soft eraser at the completion of the painting.

As pencil sketches are generally on a light-weight paper, it will be easier to paint over them if the sketch is first mounted on stiff white cardboard. Do not use glue or rubber cement—both of these adhesives will eventually stain through the paper. Instead, use a white library paste. A better adhering job will result if the paper is wet when the paste is applied. If care is exercised this can be done without smudging the penciling. Just make certain that, when pressure is applied, a sheet of clean paper is placed between the sketch and the weight used to insure a smooth and adhering surface. I suggest that you place the mounted sketch on a table, cover it with the clean sheet of paper and then put a drawing board over it. Use several books as weights and allow overnight pressure. If the sketch is small and the mounting stiff enough, little or no warping will take place. For larger sketches, a sheet of brown wrapping paper can be pasted to the back of the mounting board. This acts as a counter and prevents warping. This can be done and pressed at the same time the sketch is being mounted.

The quick on-the-spot pencil sketch, with a rough indication of the shaded areas, is shown at right.

STEP 1. *In the studio the sketch is strengthened with brush and India Ink.*

STEP 2. *Using watercolor in a transparent manner, the sketch is gradually covered with washes. At the conclusion of this step the black ink drawing is still apparent.*

STEP 3. *Now, adding Chinese White to the regular watercolors to make them opaque wherever necessary, the previously laid color washes are intensified. Some of the black ink lines are weakened or eliminated in order to impart a more atmospheric quality to the final painting. When completed, the surface of the painting is a combination of transparent and opaque color, with some of the inked lines still showing wherever they add strength or help to delineate the form of the various objects.*

CONTÉ

Conté is an excellent medium for obtaining quick, dramatic effects. It is available in stick and pencil, and both can be combined to produce the finished drawing. Black and Sanguine are the most popular colors, but other colors can be had. Sanguine and Sepia are particularly effective on a cream or ivory paper. The Black which, incidentally, was used for the drawings shown on this page, comes in three degrees—hard, medium, and soft. These are generally numbered 1, 2, and 3. Most of the work on these drawings was accomplished with the flat side of a #3 *Conté* stick. Quick, broad effects are easily arrived at by using the stick in this manner.

The drawings were done on a semitrans-parent tracing paper. I have found that a pad of such paper is very convenient for working on the spot. It can be obtained in various sizes and has a pleasant working surface. The main lines of the composition can be indicated on the top sheet, using an ordinary lead pencil. Then removing the sketch from the pad, it is placed under a fresh sheet. Enough of the preliminary penciling shows through the semitransparent sheet to act as a guide for the *Conté* rendering. This enables you to work in a much bolder and direct manner, and reduces errors in drawing. As corrections are difficult to make with this medium, the overlay method of working is of particular value.

The Conté drawing on the left served as a composition and tonal guide for the watercolor reproduced below. While it was done in the tracing pad method described above, you can work Conté on any type of drawing surface. Experiment with various surfaces but always keep a padding of paper under the surface on which you are working. This insures a more even rendering when the Conté is applied.

CRAYON

While wax crayons are seldom employed as a medium for finished pictures, you can use them in making quick color sketches. Being wax, they do not lend themselves to a smooth glossy surface. Instead, use a paper with a bit of tooth.

The chief advantage in using crayon is that it is a dry medium, and you do not have to be concerned with smearing, as is the case with pastels.

The disadvantage is in the difficulty of obtaining subtle color and tonal gradations. Crayon colors are not absolutely permanent, but as they are recommended only for the rendering of quick notes, this is not of primary concern.

On this page are reproduced examples of subject matter that lend themselves to crayon rendering. The sketch on the right was made while I was in the Armed Forces. The compactness of a box of crayon made carrying them an easy matter. A small sketch pad was the only supplementary equipment necessary. It is this convenience which makes crayons handy when traveling.

At the bottom of the page are some crayon sketches from my European notebook. They served as color notes and, together with photographs of the subject, formed valuable reference material when I developed studio paintings. You will also find crayons useful when doing watercolors. Any small area of the paper that has been covered with a heavy layer of crayon will resist the watercolor wash. You may want to employ such a device for blocking out light areas.

WATERCOLOR PENCILS

Watercolor pencils produce a stroke similar to the crayon. However, when clean water is brushed over a watercolor pencil sketch, the strokes dissolve into a color wash similar to watercolor. Although these pencils do not lend themselves to large renderings, small sketches can be produced with interesting results. They are certainly convenient to carry; they are usually packaged in a box of 24 colors.

The only additional equipment you would need is a brush and a small container of water. Sharpen the pencils so as to make a flat side on the point. Applied to the paper with the flat side, a broad stroke results. It is necessary that all of the strokes be made in an even manner in order to produce a smooth wash when moistened.

It takes some experimenting to handle watercolor pencils, because some of the colors are drastically changed when the water is applied. I find them most useful when making small studies such as those pictured on the right. The originals were twice-size. The cloud study on the top shows the effect of the pencil when left dry.

Those below have been made soluble with water.

Wherever I wanted a hard edge, I limited the use of the water. Accents can be made by using the pencil while the surface is still wet.

Shown below, on the left, the strokes of the watercolor pencil have been evenly rendered; when water is brushed over the area, a smooth wash results. The method of obtaining a hard and soft edge is shown in the S-curved line. Using a brush that has been dipped in clear water, the line is made soluble wherever desired.

When the lines are penciled unevenly and a minimum amount of water is used, a rough, uneven wash results, as illustrated directly below.

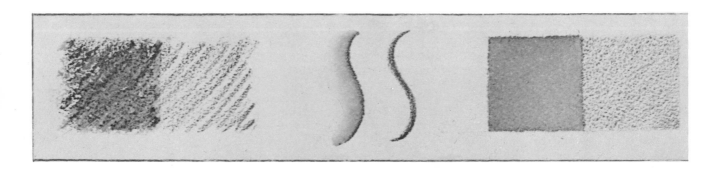

The sketch above illustrates how the application of water affects the watercolor pencil drawing. The right half of the illustration shows the original drawing before it has been moistened.

Interesting sketches can be produced by using a minimum amount of water and allowing the original penciling to show through.

PASTEL

Pastel is one of the most permanent of mediums. The chief difficulty it presents is in fixing it to keep it from smearing. While it can be sprayed with fixative at various stages, it is best to leave the final strokes untouched. The very action of a spray tends to lower the delicate color.

I have found pastel to be an excellent supplementary medium in the making of color notes. As there is no drying problem, it lends itself to quick handling of color effects. The reproduction on the right is an example of such notes. They were done on a dark gray pastel paper, each about 3 x 4 inches.

Most artists prefer soft pastels, but they are available in hard, and semihard sticks as well. Pastel paper is available in several colors. A single sheet should never be placed on the drawing board. Rather, place some extra sheets of the pastel paper or a piece of newspaper underneath the sheet you are using, in order to create a softer surface.

The preliminary drawing can be sketched in with charcoal and the latter also used for accents. Personally, I prefer to work directly

with the pastel, concentrating on effects of one color in its relationship to the other.

I do little or no work with the paper stump that is used to rub in the pastel for blending effects. I use a soft rag, or my finger occasionally, to soften a color effect. I plan the composition later in the studio and, using the pastel color notes for reference, paint the subject in watercolor or oil.

The color impression of the subject is quickly captured in pastel, working directly on the spot.

Pastel can also be used in combination with watercolor. When passages in a watercolor painting have become too dark, a few strokes of pastel over the dark area will immediately lighten them. The same applies to overworked areas. Applied in a deft manner, pastel will give these areas life.

When pastel is used as a corrective device, as in the instance above, it should be done as unobtrusively as possible. It may be necessary to rub the pastel, after it has been applied, so that it blends with the water-

color. When framed and covered with glass, the correction is hardly noticeable.

Below is an example of a watercolor that had been discarded because the contrasting values were lost, particularly in the dark areas. Using soft pastels, I proceeded to make the necessary corrections. The pastel adhered nicely to the surface, since the watercolor paper had sufficient tooth to hold the dry medium. This is an extreme example, used to illustrate my point, as the result resembled a pastel rather than a watercolor.

The unsuccessful watercolor shown on the left is salvaged with pastel as illustrated below.

WORKING FROM ON-THE-SPOT SKETCHES

I mentioned earlier that there is no substitute for on-the-spot painting. It is only after years of observing and painting directly from nature that you can do such subjects with a degree of authority in the studio. And you will constantly have to return to nature for inspiration to discover new color schemes, forms, and subject matter.

On the right is shown a small on-the-spot watercolor. Below is a large studio oil painting of the same subject. This is a basic working procedure. However, there is no reason why the spot sketch could not have been done in oil and the studio painting with watercolor. On the other hand, the same medium could be used for both the sketch and the studio painting.

What I am leading up to is that, in many of the sections on techniques, I may have indicated that a certain medium lends itself more readily to a certain type of job. That

does not mean, however, that you should limit yourself to my recommendation. The following case histories of paintings developed in the studio from on-the-spot sketches will illustrate my point.

SOME CASE HISTORIES OF STUDIO PAINTINGS

The pencil drawing on the right, with its indication of tonal values and penciled color notes, provided the plan for the watercolor shown directly below.

However, I was not satisfied with the watercolor painting. I felt that the dramatic sky and dark skyline made it top-heavy. The combination of these two elements dominated the picture, taking the viewer's interest away from the more important foreground. The lack of an integrated pattern of strong

darks and lights definitely weakened the lower half of the painting. I set to work recomposing the subject. This time the sky area was minimized, along with the extreme background area.

The middle area was redesigned and pushed back by the clouds of smoke. I then wove a strong pattern of dark shapes in the foreground, accenting them with the sharp whites of the hanging wash.

More figures were added to the composition. A strong cast shadow at the base of the painting kept the figures subordinated to the rest of the design. The telegraph pole on the right was an improvised device to hold the figures within the picture.

"Kearny Skyline"
Watercolor Prize,
Montclair Art Museum

Daylight Sketch Supplies Data for Nocturne

Of all the subject matter, it is the nocturne, especially, that requires preliminary notes and much mental observation if you are to turn out a successful studio interpretation. It is the kind of subject which seldom lends itself to painting on the spot, so you must depend on pencil notes plus your memory. In this subject I made a quick, small watercolor of the subject in daylight so that I would be certain of the details.

During a Civil Defense "alert" I spent the time observing the color effects from my window. Immediately after the "all clear" was sounded I made a watercolor study of the subject.

"City Dim-out" — Collection Philadelphia Museum

Using the daylight watercolor as a guide for the drawing, the subject was sketched on a large watercolor board. Then, referring to the color study above—plus memory—the painting was completed as shown on the right.

Summer Oil Provides Winter Watercolor

When I viewed a photographic copy of the painting reproduced on the right, I thought of it as a possible winter subject. In full color, the subject, an oil painting of a Pennsylvania summer scene, was composed of glaring rooftops. In the black and white photograph these glaring surfaces suggested snow.

I made a charcoal sketch of the subject on gray paper. Using an opaque white watercolor, I painted in snow areas. The sketch gave me some idea of the possibilities of

converting the subject into a winter scene.

Along with this conversion I decided to use a different medium. Making a pencil drawing on a sheet of heavy, rough paper I painted a watercolor of the subject. The result is shown below.

"Winter" — Collection
Springfield, Missouri Museum

113

Variations Aid Final Painting

"Black Valley" is the result of making several paintings of the same area. On the left are shown three paintings, all contributing to the final composition below.

I started with a rectangular shape, but as I worked I felt that the subject could be composed in a square shape. To fill such an uninteresting proportion was a challenge and I was anxious to see if it could be done effectively.

The painting at the lower left corner came close to a realization of what I was seeking. However, I felt that the distant hill was too similar in size and weight to the hill in the immediate area. What had first impelled me to develop the subject was also lacking—the big, dark, almost forbidding feeling of overpowering mountains. With this in mind I painted the subject once more, with the result shown below.

"Black Valley" — Palm Beach Art League Award

Change in Proportion Aids Composition

The principles stressed on page 14 are used here.

After I had completed the painting shown on the right, I was disturbed by the foreground. The automobile seemed poorly placed —it gave me the feeling of being about to fall through the base of the picture. I also thought that the shapes behind the trestle could be better designed. I repainted the picture, this time eliminating the automobile and telegraph pole and improvising a skyline for the background. While I felt that this painting was an improvement over the previous one, I still was not convinced that the design was as strong as it could be.

Starting a third time, I changed the proportions completely, working the composition into a rectangular shape. The automobile was put back into the picture but subordinated into the dark pattern on the left. The telegraph pole was also restored, but this time the dark sky prevented it from jutting out. I also felt that the dark sky helped to hold the various elements together as well as accenting the light of the snow and the building areas.

"Corner Candy Shoppe" — *Wilhelm Prize, North Shore Art Association*

Fragmentary Note Provides a Painting

There are occasions when only a fragmentary note can be obtained of a subject. In going through my sketches looking for a subject to paint, I frequently find such notes.

While I would not advise a novice to attempt to develop a painting from such slim reference, the advanced student will find it a challenging exercise. It forces him to use his resourcefulness in inventing color schemes and supplying missing details.

On this page are shown two examples of paintings developed by such means. The illustration at the bottom of the page is of particular interest, for almost the entire left side of the painting, "The Underpass," had to be improvised.

"New Hope Houses" — Washington Watercolor Club Prize

"The Underpass" — Cowie Prize,
California Watercolor Society

Ink Sketch with Color Notations Provides Studio Painting

On the left is shown an on-the-spot ink sketch. Color notations have been indicated similar to the penciled notations described in the section "Working in the Studio from Pencil Notes."

By using a fine-pointed pen, I was able to achieve a more sharply delineated line, necessary for such a subject, than I could with an ordinary lead pencil.

While I relied upon the marginal color notations, using arrows to point to the various areas, this required my marking up the sketch. I suggest the following method if you want to keep the drawing intact.

Have some sheets of tracing paper cut to the same size as the paper upon which you plan to make the drawing. After the drawing is made, clip a sheet of tracing paper over it. Then proceed to write in the various color notations on the tracing paper. The original drawing shows through clearly, act-

ing as a guide for the accurate placing of the notes. In the studio, the tracing paper overlay of notations can be keyed with the drawing for reference purposes.

An added word of caution: when writing the notations on the tracing paper overlay be careful not to indent the surface of the drawing underneath. Use a fairly soft pencil or a good ball-point pen.

The painting on the right, "The Stone Steps," was developed in the studio from the pen sketch shown above. All of the preliminary work was done with an ink undertone. When I thought I had obtained as much textural quality as possible with ink, the painting was finished with pure watercolor.

"The Stone Steps"
Parish Art Museum, Long Island

Photograph Supplies Data for Painting

I was able to make only a quick sketch of the subject shown below. As the setting was in a foreign country, it was imperative that the background material be authentic. I took a photograph of the subject, as shown at the right. While it was sadly lacking in photographic quality, it answered the purpose of recalling to mind the scene as it was when I made the sketch. Along with supplying the needed details, some of the figures in the photograph were helpful in suggesting poses that were incorporated in the final painting.

I regretted that I had not taken additional photographs, particularly a closeup of the store windows. If, when doing foreign subjects, you find it impossible to complete your sketch with all of the necessary data, it is a wise precaution to photograph several views of the subject.

"Venetian Market" — Courtesy A. Bildner

Pencil Note is Interpreted in Oil and Watercolor

Here is an example of an on-the-spot pencil sketch which provided a composition for a watercolor. I thought that the subject lent itself well to a large composition. While the watercolor was painted on a full 22 x 28 inch sheet, I stretched a 30 x 36 inch canvas and proceeded to paint the subject in oil. Some changes were made, particularly in the arrangement of the cast shadows, which I thought would improve the design.

There followed one of those occurrences that happen so rarely. The watercolor was submitted to the American Water Color Society's Annual Exhibition, where it was awarded the Obrig Prize. The oil painting was exhibited at a later date and won the Connecticut Academy Prize.

"Bealtown Road" — Obrig Prize,
American Watercolor Society

"Pennsylvania Road" — Connecticut Academy

Changing Focal Point Improves Composition

The paintings reproduced on this page are examples of how the composition can be changed by varying the point of view.

On the left, the subject has been painted from a point about 25 feet away from the nearest house. A feeling of desolation is conveyed by the untrampled snow and the lone parked automobile.

By moving closer to the subject, both the houses in the immediate foreground and the street beyond attain greater prominence. A few figures are introduced to instill a feeling of life in the subject.

By walking forward, the houses in the foreground disappear and the street beyond becomes the principal area of the composition.

These few examples will give you some idea of the various compositions that can be obtained from the same subject by just changing your focal point.

"Gloucester Street"
Philadelphia Watercolor Club Prize
Collection Philadelphia Museum

CHAPTER VII

PAINTING A MURAL FOR THE HOME

Murals for the home have become increasingly popular in the past few years. While there are many complex methods of painting murals and the art is a highly specialized one, there are some simple approaches for the easel painter.

Probably the easiest way is to do the painting in oil color on a large composition board. It can be done in the studio and then fastened to the wall. One big advantage in this method is that the panel is removable. Again, using oil paint, the mural can be made on canvas and then adhered to the wall. Although white lead, mixed with linseed oil, has been used for years as an adhesive binder to fasten the canvas to the wall, it requires experience to do a satisfactory job. (White lead is of a poisonous nature and should be handled with care.)

There is a casein-latex cement available that is much easier to handle and possesses excellent adhesive power.

The mural can also be painted directly on the plaster wall. The wall should be at least six months old and given a ground coat of white paint that is usually used for wall decorations. The surface should be absolutely dry and, if too absorbent, given a thin coating of glue size or shellac, applied before proceeding to paint the mural. Some painters use a base of white lead, ground in oil and thinned with turpentine, before starting the painting.

Casein colors can also be used and, as they are limeproof, can be painted upon either wet or dry plaster. Then dry with an attractive mat finish. This mat quality is desirable in whatever medium you use, as murals are viewed from several angles, and any reflected glare would be objectionable.

The mural shown below was painted directly on the wall with oil color.

Courtesy Mikel Stettner

WORKING PROCEDURE FOR PAINTING A MURAL

The mural shown below was painted with oil color on canvas in my studio. After it was fairly complete and dry enough to handle, I rolled and transported it loosely to the house where it was adhered to the wall. Once it was mounted, I proceeded to make color refinements I thought necessary and then painted the final details.

My working procedure in doing murals is as follows. I make a small-scale color sketch in the same proportion as the proposed mural. If the subject is one that I am familiar with, in all probability I have previously made sketches to which I can refer. If not, some research is necessary to obtain the data. As the subject, in this case a harbor scene, is a favorite of mine, I had sufficient material on hand. The source sketches for the mural are shown on the opposite page.

I took sections of these various sketches and made a composition on a sheet of water-color paper. Then, using casein paint, a rough color scheme was planned. When the color composition was satisfactory, I made a careful tracing of it, using a hard pencil. This drawing was then squared off as illustrated at the bottom of the next page.

The next step was to make a final drawing on canvas. Using charcoal, I squared off the canvas in scale to the small drawing. With the latter serving as a guide, the subject was drawn, still using charcoal on the canvas. It was then sprayed with fixative and the mural was painted.

Courtesy A. LaPoff

Instead of working from the small scale drawing shown below, you may prefer to work in the same size. A paper used by architects and known as "detail paper" is available in large rolls. The drawing can be made the actual size of the mural and the lines then perforated, (there is a perforating wheel made for this express purpose). Charcoal, or a dark chalk dust, is then pounced through the perforated holes, transferring the lines to the canvas. Another method is to have a lantern slide made of the small drawing, projecting it on the canvas to the required size.

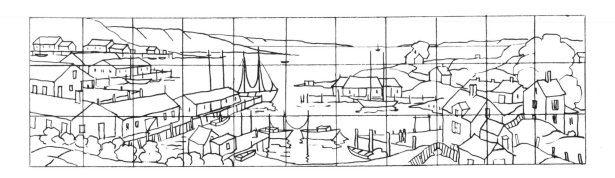

CHAPTER VIII

PICTURE PRESENTATION

While the frame on the painting may be considered merely an embellishment to the picture, its importance should not be minimized. This does not mean that an expensive frame will automatically improve the painting as a work of art. It will however, improve its appearance!

The chief offense committed by the novice seems to be in using a ready-made raw wood frame that is far too thin for the size of the oil painting he is submitting. Or, in direct contrast, he uses an ancient, heavy frame, salvaged from a second-hand shop and still retaining its original gilt or gold finish.

Now there is nothing wrong is using ready-made or old frames. But it is important that they be the right weight for the size of the painting and that they are toned to enhance the colors of the subject. Ready-made, or what are commonly called stock sized, raw wood frames can be obtained in various widths as well as in different mouldings. Just be certain to select one that is heavy enough to make your painting impressive. At the same time chose a design that makes the picture more distinctive. With some subjects, a scooped moulding that recesses the painting is preferable to a protruding design. An embellished, or more ornate frame may help a simple subject, while a detailed subject may be more effectively presented in a simple frame.

In any case, the raw wood should have some kind of finish applied over it to act as a foil and enhance the colors of the painting. Even a flat, neutral gray tone of ordinary house paint is preferable to the look of unfinished raw wood. The same point applies to the salvaged gilt frame. By merely giving it a coating of flat gray, followed by a light rubbing with steel wool to allow flecks of the original gilt to show through, an immediate improvement is made.

Many professional artists collect such old frames. In cases of excessive ornateness they remove the gingerbread with a chisel, saw, or knife. Then, by applying successive tonings of color and much rubbing, they achieve a beautiful finish.

As unfinished stock frames are available in most art supply stores and are very reasonable in price, you will undoubtedly want to experiment with them. The most popular sizes are 8 x 10, 9 x 12, 12 x 16, 16 x 20, 20 x 24 and 24 x 30 inches. Make certain that your canvases are stretched to one of these measurements so that you can take advantage of a stock size.

I have found that casein paint is excellent for obtaining a quick attractive finish. For example, by mixing White with a touch of Raw Umber a warm, gray tone is produced. It can then be applied directly to the raw wood. Before the paint dries, a textural effect can be accomplished by pouncing the wet surface with a stiff brush. Another interesting texture can be produced by running an ordinary comb over the still wet surface.

You may want to experiment with other implements to vary the surface of the frame, possibly before the paint is applied. Gouging or nicking an area of the raised surface of the frame before toning, often gives an interesting effect to an otherwise ordinary looking stock frame.

Occasions may arise when you will want to have only the best frame possible for your painting. Then take the painting to a good picture-framing shop. See what the framer has to suggest—remember that he is a specialist and has framed more pictures than you will ever possibly paint! Sometimes just a simple suggestion, like recommending a linen inset, will do wonders for your painting.

What I have had to say so far has been

directed to the framing of oil paintings, but the same principles apply to watercolors. You can, however, use lighter weight frames, and generally of a simpler design. While it is at present a popular practice to frame some watercolors the same as oil paintings, when in doubt present them simply. It takes a very strong, low-keyed watercolor to show up effectively in a narrow mat and heavy frame. It is still hard to beat the pleasing effect of a nicely proportioned white mat and simple frame!

Frames courtesy of
Rabin and Krueger,
Newark, New Jersey

Illustrated above is a ready-made raw wood frame that is too thin for the oil painting.

The appearance of the picture is immediately improved by using a heavier frame. In addition, the frame has been toned to a warm, neutral gray that enhances the colors in the painting.

The picture is further improved, particularly for exhibition purposes, by being enclosed in a still heavier frame. A linen inset adds to the effect, making it more impressive.

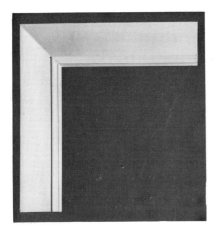 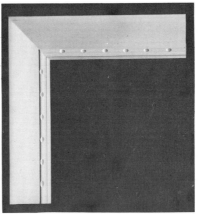  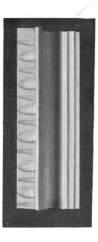

The appearance of a raw wood stock frame can often be improved by simply notching part of the frame. The illustration at the above left shows a corner of a common stock frame. A series of notches cut with a razor or X-acto blade relieves the monotony of the evenness of the raised portion of the frame. In this instance, the second illustration shows the effect of notches that were cut about one inch apart.

Another method that is not quite as simple, but very effective on a heavy frame, is to use a wood engraving tool to carve a design. The "before" and "after" effect is shown above. The thin notch is accomplished with a V-shaped tool, while a cove-shaped tool carved the alternating wide notch. It takes a little practice to be able to handle these tools, but an occasional slip may even add to the final effect!

As a general rule, the average proportioned watercolor is most pleasingly presented in a mat with equal margins on the sides and top, and with the bottom margin slightly wider. These mat measurements may also apply to watercolors that are slightly wider or deeper than those of average proportions. The matted watercolors shown below illustrate the recommended presentation.

There may be occasions when you will want to vary the mat margins. For example, a square picture can have a mat with wider margins on the side than the top or bottom. Or again, an extremely wide, but shallow in depth, picture will look attractive in a mat with the sides narrower than the top or bottom.

There are occasions when it may
be desirable to display a watercolor with a minimum amount of
mat. This is particularly applicable when hanging a watercolor
in a home where wall space is
limited.

Or again, a toned or linen mat
may aid in carrying out the color
scheme of the room. Such a mat,
made in the proportions previously described, may overwhelm
the picture.

As shown above, a minimum
amount of white mat is displayed,
along with a white frame. A
rather anemic look results. On the
left is the same picture, but the
frame has been toned, and a linen
mat aids in contributing to the
over-all harmonious effect. The
narrow white border between the
mat and the painting helps to
avoid a "heavy look" and gives
the picture a lift.

Gouache and casein paintings can
often be displayed to advantage
in a heavy frame. Generally, unlike the light, airy look of transparent watercolors, their strong,
opaque qualities are similar, vis-
ually, to oil paintings and can
be framed accordingly. If the
casein paintings are varnished
or waxed, the glass can be
eliminated.

It is important that the frame be toned harmoniously with the picture. On the above left, the dead white frame contrasts too severely with the dark subject. By toning the frame to a darker, neutral tint with casein paint, the over-all effect is more harmonious.

In the section "Emphasis through Size and Shape" mention was made of salvaging a watercolor by cropping. Below is an interesting case of salvaging not only the original painting, but getting another picture out of the cropped area! The subject was a market place, with the usual colorful street stalls and people milling about. I felt that the strong light striking the tops of the buildings drew the viewer's attention away from the center of interest. My first thought was to repaint these areas in a lower key. However, by experimenting with the "L" shaped mats I decided to eliminate the top area entirely. Upon trimming the painting I noted the discarded area and thought it had possibilities as a picture complete in itself. I touched it up a bit and had it framed as shown below.